"Looking for a bridge to the future? Take this one. When churches build a bridge by starting in the middle, the end result is a bridge to nowhere. Jimmy Long has traveled both sides, knows the depth of the chasm that separates the banks of established churches from emerging ones, and is conversant in the current conversations on either side of the scholarly divides. This book will help you be a bridgebuilder in your church, your family and your community."

Leonard Sweet, author of *The Church of the Perfect Storm* and *The Gospel According to Starbucks*

"An extremely timely book that just might save the established church. Long describes in detail one of the most urgent and potentially destructive issues of our time—how to transition leadership from the top-down, command-and-control world of modernity to the bottom-up, team-based, permission-giving, emerging postmodern world. He not only casts a vision for intergenerational partnerships, but he also gives practical tools for accomplishing the vision. Kudos on you Jimmy."

Bill Easum, author of *Leadership on the Other Side,* and cofounder, Easum, Bandy & Tenny-Brittian

"For more than three decades, Jimmy Long has worked day in and day out to cultivate leaders. He has mentored dozens of them. Scores of them. Hundreds of them! He watched them, generation by generation, pass through their early adult years as their leadership took form. What he learned from them he kept in critical dialogue with the styles and instincts of their predecessors. I can't imagine anyone in as unique a position to provide the bridges we need for partnership in the midst of contending and changing leadership models alive today in the church."

George R. Hunsberger, professor of missiology, Western Theological Seminary, and coordinator, the Gospel and Our Culture Network

"Our culture is rapidly changing. And that includes how leaders think, behave and relate to one another across the generational divide in the church. Jimmy Long has done an amazing job in providing practical help in how to navigate the emerging leadership landscape. The younger leaders I work with will wish that every senior leader would read this book with them."

Stephen Hayner, professor of church growth, Columbia Theological Seminary

"The legacy of baby-boomer pastors depends on their willingness to empower the next generation of church leaders. Likewise, the effectiveness of younger pastors depends on their willingness to learn from the wisdom of their elders. Jimmy Long is one of the best-qualified voices to speak to both sides, and his book helps leaders believe, perhaps for the first time, that the generation gap can be overcome. *The Leadership Jump* is a valuable read for every church wrestling with generational transition."

Skye Jethani, managing editor, *Leadership Journal,* and author of *The Divine Commodity: Discovering a Faith Beyond Consumer Christianity*

"For decades, Christian leadership has been stuck retro-cartoonland: vision-slinging heros, lone-rangers and clip-art maps of the world. Long shifts us into hyper-speed with this one. No asteroid unturned."

Sally Morgenthaler, author, *Worship Evangelism*

"I would love to put *The Leadership Jump* into the hands of existing leaders of the first-generation congregation and emerging leaders of the English ministry of every ethnic church in the country. In my fifteen years of working closely with both groups in Asian American churches, there's been a need for a resource to get the two sides talking constructively. Jimmy Long's book would fill this void well."

Paul Tokunaga, author of *Invitation to Lead: Guidance for Emerging Asian American Leaders*

THE
LEADERSHIP
JUMP

Building Partnerships Between Existing
and Emerging Christian Leaders

JIMMY LONG

An imprint of InterVarsity Press
Downers Grove, Illinois

InterVarsity Press
P.O. Box 1400, Downers Grove, IL 60515-1426
World Wide Web: www.ivpress.com
E-mail: email@ivpress.com

InterVarsity Press® is the book-publishing division of InterVarsity Christian Fellowship/USA®, a student movement active on campus at hundreds of universities, colleges and schools of nursing in the United States of America, and a member movement of the International Fellowship of Evangelical Students. For information about local and regional activities, write Public Relations Dept., InterVarsity Christian Fellowship/USA, 6400 Schroeder Rd., P.O. Box 7895, Madison, WI 53707-7895, or visit the IVCF website at <www.intervarsity.org>.

All Scripture quotations, unless otherwise indicated, are taken from the Holy Bible, Today's New International Version™ Copyright © 2001 by International Bible Society. All rights reserved.

Design: Cindy Kiple

Images: ripped jeans: Gustaf Brundin/iStockphoto
        suit material: Roman Peregontsev/iStockphoto

ISBN 978-0-8308-3364-1

Printed in the United States of America ∞

Library of Congress Cataloging-in-Publication Data

Long, Jimmy.
  The leadership jump: building partnerships between existing and
  emerging Christian leaders / Jimmy Long.
      p. cm.
  Includes bibliographical references.
  ISBN 978-0-8308-3364-1 (pbk.: alk. paper)
  1. Christian leadership. 2. Intergenerational relations—Religious
  aspects—Christianity. 3. Intergenerational communication—Religious
  aspects—Christianity. 4. Leadership—Religious
  aspects—Christianity.   I. Title.
  BV652.1.L655 2008
  253—dc22

                                                                    2008039555

P   24   23   22   21   20   19   18   17   16   15   14   13   12   11   10   9   8   7   6   5   4   3   2   1

Y   29   28   27   26   25   24   23   22   21   20   19   18   17   16   15   14   13   12   11   10   09

To Steve Hayner,
 who initially provided me
 the opportunity to write in this area

To Dieter Zander,
 who was the first person
 who encouraged me to write a book on leadership

Contents

Part One

CHANGING CULTURE, CHANGING LEADERSHIP

The Leadership Dilemma

EXISTING TO EMERGING LEADERS

Question to ponder:
What is the leadership dilemma we face today?

I laughed so I wouldn't cry! Within twenty-four hours I had met with two of my best friends, Jonathan and Ken, who both happened to be pastors in a church I know well. First, I met with Jonathan, the senior pastor, in his church office. He wondered aloud to me, "What does Ken do all day? All I see him do is sit in Starbucks talking all day with people from the church and the community. What are his plans and programs to move his ministry forward?"

The next day I sat down with Ken at (where else?) Starbucks. Without my mentioning my previous day's conversation with Jonathan, Ken began to wonder out loud also. "Jonathan spends so much time on plans and programs for the church that he rarely takes the time to sit down and get to know the church staff or other people in the church. The church staff do not seem to know Jonathan or fully trust him."

Those two conversations summed up for me the dilemma we are facing in the church, other Christian organizations and the corporate world to some degree. We have two significantly conflicting views of who a leader is and what a leader does. Do we focus on people or programs? Do we put our energy toward fulfilling plans or developing relationships? These conversations were not the first time I felt caught in the middle between two conflicting groups.

As I have traveled to church leadership seminars throughout this country in the last ten years, I have had numerous conversations about leadership differences with younger and older ministry leaders. It does not matter whether these leaders are in the church, a parachurch ministry, college administration or the business world. What I have found out is that we are facing a major divergence of views on who a leader is and what a leader does as we are running headlong into this emerging culture—some of us kicking and screaming, while others of us are celebrating and rejoicing. The difference in leadership views is not primarily an age difference but instead is a cultural difference caused by this change from a modern to a postmodern or emerging culture.

The result is that we are facing a leadership dilemma. As we have now moved well into the twenty-first century, many in the church are concerned about the moral dilemma outside the church. Others are concerned about the theological dilemma within the church. I think the biggest dilemma the church is facing is a leadership dilemma.

Where Have All the Leaders Gone?

A few years ago I chuckled when I first saw the commercial where young boys and girls are asked what they aspire to be when they grow up. A number of them say they want to be a middle manager. I initially thought that commercial was cute. However, after seeing the commercial a couple of times, my chuckles turned to sadness. Although the commercial was trying to be cute, it had touched on a real concern today. Where have all the leaders gone?

When I was growing up, most of the people around me had aspirations to lead. I knew many young people who, when asked, "What do you want to be when you grow up?" answered that they aspired to some type of leadership role, such as president of the United States, a general in the army, pastor of a church or head of their own business. When I was younger, I wanted to be a meteorologist who would tame hurricanes. People aspired to be leaders. People wanted to change the world! Those aspirations have changed in a few short decades.

Today, all over the world, people are realizing we have a crisis in leadership. There is a growing, pervasive belief that we are facing a shortage of leaders capable of leading organizations into the future. Ninety-seven percent of organizations report significant shortages of leadership. Forty percent of organizations view this gap as acute. Close to 75 percent of companies report this leadership gap as having a modest to significant negative impact on the company's productivity.[1] As I have traveled to many seminaries, I have found that students in seminary want to be teachers, counselors and pastors. Few want to be church leaders. Furthermore, most seminaries are expending little energy training students to become leaders.

The early twenty-first century is not the first time people have been reluctant to lead. Even God has had a hard time in the past inspiring people to lead. Moses, probably the most important Hebrew leader, did not want to lead. In Exodus 3:10–4:18 we have the privilege to listen in on the conversation God and Moses had about leadership. Moses tried every excuse he could think of for why he should not lead. First, he tried to say he was inadequate. "Who am I that I should go to Pharaoh and bring the Israelites out of Egypt?" (Ex 3:11). After God answered that excuse, Moses said he did not think he had enough authority for the Israelites to listen to him. He gave excuse after excuse until finally he told God to send some-one else. "Pardon your servant, Lord. Please send someone else" (4:13). At last, when Moses agreed to go, he told his father-in-law, "Let me return to my own people in Egypt to see if any of them are still alive" (4:18). One could build a case that Moses was the most reluctant leader of all time.

Why is the desire to be a leader dropping significantly again? In the corporate world, middle management jobs are falling out of favor fast. Also, fewer people want to be the boss. These jobs are seen as a negative because they require long hours with little re-ward. Leadership positions—previously a career goal for many—are being shunned by today's workers. There is loyalty neither to their boss nor to their company. Modern leaders were reared with a commitment to company loyalty and an understanding of hier-archy. They realized that they needed to pay their dues as they as-cended the corporate ladder. Part of the reason for the lessening interest in leadership positions is the distrust in leadership today. People do not want to be part of the distrusted leadership team. Also, for emerging leaders, climbing the corporate or church lad-der is not their view of success.

A shortage of leaders is also appearing at this time because the world is still reeling from an environment of failed leadership. These failures are due to many reasons. They have come because leaders have too few resources, too much bureaucracy, too much autonomy, too much control. In response to this turbulent environment, leaders have either just called it quits or have grasped for too much power.[2]

In the past, companies like IBM retained leaders for a lifetime because of a deep loyalty and commitment between the company and its employees. Organizations fostered a culture of loyalty and a corporate paternalism. However, as these companies have needed to change because of changing economic and cultural conditions, the loyalty tie significantly weakened. It is no different in the church or other ministry organizations. The strong ties of the past have now been seriously weakened. There is no longer a reciprocal loyalty between church and pastoral staff.

The Widening Gap

Also, whether in the corporate world or ministry world, there is a widening gap between the older (existing) leaders and the younger (emerging) leaders. The existing leaders do not see the emerging leaders as being willing to carry their load. Many existing leaders do not see the emerging leaders as being in any hurry to take on leadership roles. Other present leaders are seeing leadership roles being offered to emerging leaders and cannot understand how these emerging leaders are turning down these job offers. They wonder if the emerging leaders just do not have the drive they have, are satisfied in the role they presently have or fear they will be less successful in a more senior position.

Many emerging leaders feel stifled because they come into leadership roles in existing churches, where all the questions of how to organize and how to lead were answered long ago. They do not feel that there is any room or openness for new ways of leading. This is why they are leaving the existing churches or businesses to start their own church or business. As Tim Keel, one of the emerging church leaders, has recently stated, "Creative types are often unwilling to navigate labyrinthine administrative structures in order to get permission to do something they could easily do on their own."[3]

Not only are emerging leaders reluctant to take leadership positions but also, where existing and emerging leaders are working together, there is a lack of understanding of how to collaborate. In a recent survey of corporate leaders, 40 percent concluded that they had been unsuccessful in getting older, existing leaders and younger, emerging leaders to collaborate.[4]

Since these two groups do not automatically think alike, there are a growing number of situations where they are struggling to know how to work together. This tension and lack of understanding of each other can escalate quickly. In the weeks following my conversations with Jonathan and Ken, their tension with each other rapidly increased. How do leaders deal with this kind of tension? For a growing number of emerging leaders, they just leave. I have met numerous emerging church leaders who have left their present church staff position, or wished they could leave, because of significant differences with the existing senior pastor or other senior staff leaders on how to lead.

Furthermore, only 40 percent of managers are satisfied with their boss. I wonder how many emerging church leaders are satisfied with their senior pastor? A recent study noted that more than two-thirds of the people who leave their jobs do so because of a bad working relationship with their boss.[5] From their perspective, the boss may be ineffective and incompetent. Minimally, their boss does not understand them. So these emerging leaders, when they leave, do not leave the organization as much as they quit their boss. The existing leader who has the power and the emerging leader who has new ideas of how to lead just cannot seem to work together or learn how to lead together. The result is that instead of existing and emerging leaders learning how to partner together, they are parting ways. How can we reverse the trend so that, instead of parting ways, existing and emerging leaders can build partnerships?

New Types of Leaders

There is a desperate need for new types of leaders. These new types of leaders have to both invent the future and deal with the past. They will need to work in new ways. However, there is no manual yet to show how this new leadership needs to act. It has yet to be developed. So these new leaders must at the same time "invent new processes and organizing forms, and simultaneously solve the complex problems of this time."[6]

As we all know, it is difficult to break with the traditions, history and familiar patterns of the past. It is also not easy to establish new traditions. Our church, which is located in the college town of Chapel Hill, North Carolina, is in the midst of learn-

> We need leaders who know how to nourish and rely on their innate creativity, freedom, generosity, and caring of people. We need leaders who are life affirming rather than life destroying. Unless we quickly figure out how to nurture and support the new leadership, we can't hope for peaceful change.
>
> MARGARET WHEATLEY
> *Finding Our Way*

ing how to transition from being a church that was very modern to being a church that knows how to minister in this emerging culture. We are learning how to lead a church that is transitioning from focusing on a modern, older constituency that does not want much change to a younger group of people who are demanding the church change how it does ministry within this emerging culture. How are we going to be able to lead the church in this new environment?

From Existing to Emerging Leaders

As we continue to move into this emerging culture, we will need both existing leaders, who understand the old patterns of leadership, and emerging leaders, who can eventually bring about new patterns of leadership. Existing leaders will have to be willing to give up their stability and the predictability of the past. We must empower the emerging leaders who are not tied to the past way of doing leadership and are not afraid to develop new ways of leading. If the emerging leaders were honest with us, they would admit that they already feel insecure within the existing leadership structure because it does not meet their needs or the needs of the emerging culture.

We are in the early stages of this massive transition. Existing and emerging leaders should find a common ground so they can work together to discover the future in the midst of a present where there are few clear answers or complete solutions. Existing leaders will need to be willing to give up control and empower the emerging leaders to lead the church into and through the emerging culture. How will this change of leadership take place? What will this new form of leadership look like?

The Leadership Jump

In the past I would have described this change of leadership as the handing off of the baton, like one would do in a relay race. However, the more I have thought about it, the more I have realized that a baton exchange is not a helpful analogy. In a relay race the first runner hands the baton to the next runner, who runs around the same track and just hopes to run faster than the previous runner. He does the same thing only faster. As we move into this emerging culture, we who are existing leaders and we who are emerging leaders need to recognize that we will not be leading the same way. Leadership and all other types of ministry will look different than they did before— sometimes radically different. If we want to use the racing analogy, we might imagine a biathlon where we move from running to swimming. However, even that analogy is lacking.

I would rather describe this leadership transition as a jump. In my previous book, *Emerging Hope,* I employ a meteorological analogy, referring to the two wind patterns in hurricanes to describe the interplay between generational transition and cultural transition.[7] I think there is another weather analogy that might be helpful to depict the leadership partnership and transition from existing to emerging leaders. The leadership handover is less a transition or evolution into something new than a transference or redirection. Let me describe what I mean.

Birth of a Nor'easter

During the winter in the eastern United States, one of the most powerful weather occurrences is the nor'easter storm, which dumps lots of snow in New England. When I was in seminary at Gordon-Conwell's Massachusetts campus in the early 1970s, I was the recipient of numerous nor'easters. When I moved to North

Carolina to go on InterVarsity staff at UNC Chapel Hill, I moved
closer to the origination point of the storms off the North Carolina
coast. So I have seen up close and personal both the origination and
the results of nor'easters.

What people do not realize is that nor'easters are formed primarily in two ways. The calmer nor'easters gradually form off the
North Carolina coast and slowly move up the coast, producing a
reasonable amount of snow. However, the massive nor'easters usually form from the energy transference from a dying storm west of
the Appalachian Mountains to a fledgling storm off the Carolina
coast. The first storm heads east from the Midwest, or northeast
from Texas, and runs into the Appalachian Mountains. Since it does
not have the strength to move over the mountains, the storm has
two options. It can either die a slow death west of the Appalachian
Mountains or see its energy center jump over the mountains to empower the fledgling nor'easter off the Carolina coast.

One of the main reasons a storm center jumps is that the upper-
level energy, which supports the storm, moves past the primary
storm's location. The present storm no longer has the energy to
continue to push itself over the mountains into a new environment.
Therefore, instead of knocking itself against the mountains and
eventually dying, the center of energy jumps over the mountains
to empower the new storm that is in a much more favorable environment for growth. This energy-center jump provides the fuel for
the new storm to grow rapidly and move up the coast with much
greater energy than it could have if it had to produce all its own
energy without any help from the original storm west of the Appalachians. Eventually the original storm dies, but only after giving
its energy to this emerging storm off the coast.

Future Leadership Options

This analogy provides a valuable example of how leadership transference can, and I think should, happen between existing and emerging leaders. There is no doubt that over the coming years there will be a leadership transfer from existing to emerging leaders. There are three primary options for how this leadership transfer can take place. One option could be that existing leaders will try to hand over the leadership to leaders who are committed to doing leadership like their predecessors. This leadership will be severely handicapped because they will be trying to lead in an emerging culture using leadership principles and tactics that were designed for a former culture.

A second option is that emerging leaders will leave the existing church and try to develop an emerging ministry using only emerging leadership. They might succeed but will not have all the resources or wisdom they need, similar to the nor'easter that forms without the energy from the storm west of the Appalachians. Also, this option means the existing church will eventually die out and not make the transition into the emerging culture.

The best solution is for the existing leaders to bless and empower the emerging leaders to make a leadership jump, realizing that the way the emerging leaders will lead will be different from that of their predecessors. This blessing and empowerment will provide the emerging leaders with all the resources they require from the past and all the freedom they will need for the future to lead the church in the emerging culture.

How do you go about making a successful leadership jump? This book is an attempt to develop an understanding and process to make this leadership jump successful. The result, I hope, will be a healthy and vibrant church initially led by a partnership of existing leaders who possess the wisdom of the past and emerging leaders who are able to exercise their creativity in the present to develop the powerful church of the future. How do we jump from a church that is presently led by existing leaders to a church that in the future is led primarily by emerging leaders? To begin, we will look at this cultural jump from the modern to emerging culture. As we understand this transition and how change takes place, then we will be better prepared to lead our church through this leadership jump.

Changes to Consider

1. Conduct a frank discussion between your church's existing and emerging leaders to discover how your leadership views are similar or different.

2. Assess how well your senior leaders and younger leaders presently partner together.

3. What possible changes do you need to make in your leadership structure to create an environment for future change?

The Church's Dilemma

MODERN TO EMERGING CULTURE

Question to ponder:
In what ways do your church and church leadership
need to change to be better prepared to minister
and lead in this emerging culture?

In the late 1990s I was invited to participate in a conference at Trinity Evangelical Divinity School titled "Telling the Truth: Evangelizing Postmoderns." As I met a few months before the conference with Dr. Donald Carson and the two other professors who were helping to lead the conference, I asked them why they titled the conference with that particular name. I went on to share with them some of my concerns about the name. The name seemed to me to indicate that we as evangelicals could and should stand outside the postmodern world to share the gospel with postmoderns. It was almost like we did not want to get tainted with postmodern culture. The name of the conference also indicated that all we needed to do to evangelize postmoderns was to tell the truth. We seemed to not

want to get involved in the lives of these postmoderns but rather
to stand at a distance while we told them the truth. The seminary
leaders politely listened to my concerns but did not fully agree with
me. As I left that discussion, I wondered how we could adequately
share the gospel without standing in the midst of the emerging culture and caring for people's needs within it.

My concerns played themselves out on my trip from O'Hare Airport to Trinity the day the conference began. I began asking questions of Jane, the limousine driver whom the seminary had hired
to pick me up and take me to the conference. I discovered quickly
that Jane wanted to talk. She told me that she was twenty-five,
was engaged to be married and had a six-year-old son. She was es-
tranged from her family. They never said they loved her and so she
didn't connect emotionally with her family. She got involved in a
relationship, which didn't go well, became pregnant and gave birth
to a child out of wedlock. Now, six years later, she was engaged to
be married to somebody who was thirty-five and had his own ten-
year-old child. She was determined to marry only once.

I allowed her to share her story. When Jane dropped me off, she
thanked me for listening to her story. She said that she had driven
two other groups of people to the conference and when she had
gotten to the point where she mentioned having a six-year-old child
but not being married, the conversation ended.

If we are going to do ministry in this emerging culture, we
cannot stand outside the culture like the name of the conference
suggested or like the other passengers whom Jane met on the trip
from the airport tried to do. If we are going to minister or lead effectively, we will want to lead from within and not from without.
For the existing leaders, we should make sure we understand this
emerging culture. For those of us who are emerging leaders, we

need to understand where the church has been so we can partner with existing leaders to lead our churches out of a modern cultural context into an emerging cultural context.

The Changing World Around Us

The world is changing around us so fast that we can hardly keep up with the changes. If we want to realize how rapidly this world is changing, we can consider the evolution of how we listen to music. I grew up with records made of vinyl. Records were followed in succession by eight-track tapes, cassettes, CDs and now iPods, all in the span of thirty years. Thomas Friedman, in his book *The Lexus and the Olive Tree,* states that the postmodern world is just about twenty years old. From his perspective this new emerging culture had its birth on November 9, 1989, with the tearing down of the Berlin Wall, marking the end of the Cold War. The wall was the symbol of the Cold War.[1] If the wall was the symbol of the Cold War, the Web is the symbol of the emerging culture. The Berlin Wall represented the armed-fortress mentality of the Cold War. The Web represents the boundary-free world of the emerging culture.

In the modern world, symbolized by the Cold War, life was compartmentalized, regimented and strictly organized. Leadership in the corporate world and the church was highly regimented. For several centuries, leadership was defined by industrial society. We were in the business of producing and making things. Leaders defined themselves as managers. Authority in the modern world was based upon rules, roles and organizational structures. Carl Raschke calls the modern church a "managed faith body." Leadership was based upon reason, and the leader followed the plan.[2] The result is that many existing leaders represent the hierarchical and controlling view of leadership.

The emerging culture is much more open, with few restrictions and unlimited opportunities. Bill Gates says, "The only factory asset we have is the human imagination."[3] If the modern leader is represented by hierarchy and directing, the emerging leader is represented by a "culture of networking, permission giving and empowerment."[4] There are many resources available to give us a more thorough understanding of this change from modern to emerging culture.[5]

Giving Up the Certainty of the Past

For many of us, especially if we are older, this changing world frightens us. Many evangelical Christians see this world filled with chaos, confusion and complexity. They hunker down in their Christian subculture and hold on to their traditions from the past. They come out of their enclaves only for short periods of time. Len Sweet describes the type of mission work they do as "search and rescue missions."[6] Much of the content of the evangelism conference at Trinity was couched as a search-and-rescue mission. The types of people these churches attract are those who want a "safe" church experience where things will stay the same. Alan Roxburgh depicts this type of church as a "ghetto of a certain socio-economic group, not an outpost of the kingdom."[7] People in these churches want a gated community church.

On the other hand, many of us who are younger or part of the emerging church movement see this emerging culture as an opportunity to make great changes in the church and in society. Many emerging leaders think we need to fundamentally change the way we do church. We will have to rethink our old assumptions. Instead of withdrawing from the culture, emerging leaders are calling churches to be people of compassion and agents of change within the community. Emerging leaders are building partnerships with Christian and community organizations that are trying to care for the people in the community.

Those of us who want to make significant changes in how we live out our faith in the emerging culture are frightening many of the existing leaders. Many of us, including those of us who are leaders, when we are frightened and confused, tend to go back to our default mode, where we feel most comfortable.

As church leaders grow older, many are afraid of the unknown. Bill Easum has learned, through his many years of training church leaders, that "people who become comfortable with the present learn to live in the past. The last thing they want to do is to introduce the future into their environment."[8] As the world becomes more chaotic and people question both the meaning

> Our actions are most likely to revert to what is habitual when we are in a state of fear or anxiety. . . . Even as conditions in the world change dramatically, most businesses, governments, schools, and other large organizations, driven by fear, continue to take the same kinds of institutional actions that they always have. . . . At best, we get better at what we have always done. We remain secure in the cocoon of our own worldview, isolated from the larger world.
>
> PETER M. SENGE, C. OTTO SCHARMER, JOSEPH JAWORSKI AND BETTY SUE FLOWERS
> *Presence*

and the meaninglessness of life, they are searching for leaders who will rescue them from this uncertain world. They want leaders to end this uncertainty, to make things better and to create stability. Too often we only think about what is best for us. However, we also should ask what God wants not only *for* us but *of* us.

The Early Church's Dilemma

We certainly are not the first church leaders who have faced the dilemma of how to minister in a different culture. What if the early church leaders only wanted to maintain the status quo? Where would the church be today? Actually, the early church leaders came close to just being a Jewish sect.

The apostle Peter, powerful leader that he was, certainly had strong ideas of how Jesus should act and how the church should function after Jesus ascended to heaven. As Peter faced the Gentile culture in Acts 10, his first response was to act the same as if he were in a Jewish culture. Although Peter was open to Gentiles entering the church, the ground rules for entrance remained the same as if they were from a Jewish culture. He initially advocated that the church continue the policy of requiring all male converts, including Gentile males, to be circumcised in order to be part of the church. In other words, the Gentiles were allowed to be part of the church but only if they came into the church under Jewish terms and Jewish traditions. Peter was satisfied with the status quo.

However, as Peter entered into this Gentile culture, which was definitely outside his comfort zone, he began to be open to the possibility that he might be wrong. Certainly he had some assistance—a vision from God in a dream—in seeing the error of his views. Peter began to realize that God might want the church to work differently in a non-Jewish culture. Instead of requiring Gentiles enter the church with a continuation of the Jewish tradition, Peter began to understand that God was calling the church to do ministry in a radically new way as it entered into a new culture. So, first, Peter had to change. However, that was not enough. Next, although Peter finally grasped what God was calling the church to do, he had to spend a long period of time convincing the rest of the leadership council of the necessity of change.

What if Peter had not grasped that God was calling the church to radical change? What if he had not been able to convince the rest of the leadership team to see that God was calling the church into a radical new way of doing ministry? How would the early church have been different? As the church moved into new cultures throughout history, it has always had the choice either to continue doing ministry as it had in a previous culture or else to be willing to do ministry differently because of the new cultural context. The church has flourished as it has been willing to adapt to new cultural contexts while remaining committed to the gospel. Are we at another crossroads today? If we are, it will be leaders like Peter who have to change first.

Leaders' Willingness to Change for the Future

Before leaders can encourage change to take place in others, they themselves, like Peter, have to be willing to change. Leaders will need to let go of their present understanding and fixed attitudes. In the midst of our change and the change we are asking others around us to make, leaders will need a high tolerance for uncertainty and confusion. Existing leaders are not being asked to become postmodern but rather to recognize that the context we are ministering within has changed. We are

> It is not easy leading in the emerging church. We face many issues which didn't exist in prior generations. If we are motivated by the desire to build a big church or to create a safe subculture for Christians, or if we tend to believe that "these emerging generations just don't get it and probably never will," then we're in big trouble. We will become incredibly frustrated. We truly need to be motivated, like Jesus, by a broken heart.
>
> DAN KIMBALL
> *The Emerging Church*

facing an emerging culture in which both existing and emerging leaders must admit that they do not know how to proceed.

Existing and emerging leaders should recognize that some of this cultural change might be from God's initiative. God was definitely involved in bringing about the church's move into the Gentile world. Not only did the church have an outreach into the Gentile culture, but also it radically changed some of its traditions and strategies as it immersed itself in the Gentile culture. The church did not have a search-and-rescue mission into the Gentile culture, but its existing and emerging leaders in partnership with each other led the church into the Gentile context. And the early church period was certainly not the only time God took initiative to galvanize his people into moving into new cultures. In the *Emerging Culture Curriculum Kit* we produced a video titled

God's Work Through History, which documents how God has been involved in much of the significant cultural changes to bring about his purposes.[9] As we look back in history, we see how God has been involved in such cultural transitions as the exodus, the Babylonian captivity, the Pax Romana and the Reformation. How does God want his church involved in this new cultural change? The existing and emerging leaders need each other in determining how God wants his church involved as we move further into the emerging culture.

Partnering Together: Leading the Change

The long-term success of an existing or emerging leader of an organization or church depends on the leader's ability to understand the times and lead the organization into the emerging culture. It isn't necessary to fear the change, but we can see the change as an opportunity God is providing us to effect the change he wants to bring. Peter Drucker, one of the leading Christian business leaders of the twentieth century, describes the position we should take as follows: "You have to infuse your entire organization with the mindset that change is an opportunity and not a threat."[10] As leaders help their churches or organizations through this cultural change, three critical questions to ask are these:

1. How is culture changing?

2. How is God involved in this cultural change?

3. How does God want us to be involved?

As people who believe God is sovereign, we should not fear change but rather should ask how God is involved in this changing culture and how he wants us to respond. We should be at the forefront of the cultural changes if God is involved. Instead of being the last to change, we should be leading the change if God is involved. God is calling us to anticipate the changes and to try to keep up with them. Erwin McManus, a leading emerging pastor, declares, "My goal is not to keep up with the changing world, but to be standing there waiting for it when it arrives. People are going to need someone to show them the way."[11]

Change Led by Emerging Leaders

Erwin McManus is correct that people do need others to show them the way. Also, we have to recognize that true change usually begins at the local, not national, leadership level. "Life's process for change is termed *emergence*," says Margaret Wheatley. "In nature, change never happens as a result of top-down, preconceived strategic plans or from the mandate of any single individual or boss. Change almost always begins as local actions spring up simultaneously around the system."[12]

In the West we should recognize that the church, as it moves into the emerging culture, will need to be eventually led by young, emerging leaders. As we think about major cultural transitions in the past, many of them were led by young leaders. Martin Luther posted the Ninety-Five Theses when he was just thirty-four years old. In the twentieth century Martin Luther King Jr. led the Montgomery bus boycott, which was the beginning of the civil rights movement, at the age of twenty-seven.

Learning Together

Older existing leaders should recognize that they must both unlearn old habits and learn new strategies if they are going to be successful leaders in the emerging culture. As Eddie Gibbs explains, "The ministry training I received over forty years ago was for a world that now no longer exists. . . . Consequently, the major challenge for leaders is not only the acquisition of new insights and skills but also unlearning what they already know."[13] The first step in this process is willingness to change.

While there might be some leaders who wonder if the journey into change is worth it, there are many existing and emerging leaders who are wandering around knowing that they are not the leaders they want to be and not the leaders the people they are leading deserve. Many of the older and younger leaders recognize that something has to change. They recognize that the old ways of leading do not work. They know they must let go of the predictable past and embrace the unpredictable future.

Many of the emerging leaders are weary of fighting battles with the existing leaders they work with in the church. Instead of concentrating on where the church has been, they want to concentrate on what the church should be and where it should go. The emerging leaders have only known change and are tired of trying to convince the existing leaders of the necessity of change. They will either stay in the church to work for change or leave the church to start their own emerging churches.

Both existing and emerging leaders feel alone and uncertain of what the future holds. Both sets of leaders need each other to overcome their fears and ease their uncertainty about the future. They will need to look to the future together. Existing leaders should listen to emerging leaders to help interpret the culture and lead them into an imaginative future. Emerging leaders should be patient and not just immediately run away from existing churches and institutions. They will need to receive from the existing leaders a sense of history and tradition. Both existing and emerging leaders will have to listen to each other.

Prerequisites for Change: Listen and Understand

We in the church have a historical example of the necessity of listening and understanding. In the process of transferring leadership from Saul to David, more than two hundred leaders of the tribe of Issachar met with David and were commended because they understood their times (1 Chron 12:32). This understanding led them to prepare for the future. If we fail to understand our present times, then we will provide leadership not for the present but for the past. One of the first changes to make as leaders, and to help our constituents make, is to let go of our certainty and our current views of how leadership works so we can develop a new understanding of what is going on.

It is ironic from Charles Handy's perspective that "every generation perceives itself as justifiably different from its predecessor, but plans as if its successor generation will be the same."[14] The ability to understand today's times and project what the future may hold is what separates the truly great from the merely compe-

> **Much has been said about the need for vision in leaders, but too little has been said of their need to listen, to absorb, to search the environment for trends, and to build the organization's capacity to learn. . . . We may have made it difficult for the learning leader to admit that his or her vision is not clear and that the whole organization together will have to learn.**
>
> EDWARD SCHEIN
> *Organizational Culture and Leadership*

tent. George Hunsberger describes these great leaders as "leaders who possess a discerning historical memory and an expectant future perspective."[15] Existing and emerging leaders need each other to make sure we connect the perspective of the past with the hopes of the future.

As we begin to understand our times, we can then proceed into the uncertain future. As the church is faced with moving further into the emerging culture, it has three options. First, it can try to retreat to the glory of the past and pretend that nothing has changed. Second, it can freely adopt all the attributes of the emerging culture and thus be assimilated into it. Or third, it can continue on its journey into this emerging-culture context looking to God for guidance.

Some of the existing leaders of the church today long for the "glory days" of the recent past. As Dorothy exclaimed in the *Wizard of Oz,* "We're not in Kansas anymore!" You cannot return to something that no longer exists. Today's emerging leaders fear that the existing leaders and existing churches want to retreat to a past that no longer exists. They want to reminisce more about the past than to dream about the future.

> **Howard Hendricks** often said, **"When your memories are more exciting than your dreams, you've begun to die."** Healthy churches must continue to find their greatest joy in their dreams, not in their memories. May those dreams call us to life-giving innovation.
>
> **H. DALE BURKE**
> "Even Healthy Churches Need to Change"

Some existing leaders fear that the emerging leaders are choosing the second option. They fear that the emerging leaders are selling out to the emerging culture. They are becoming emerging churches absorbed by the culture, instead of being churches planted in the emerging culture yet distinct from the culture.

The third option before us is to continue together into the future by seeking God's guidance. What God is calling the church to do is not to retreat to the past or to be content with the present but to move into the future, not knowing exactly what the future will hold. It is only through existing and emerging leaders partnering together that can we lead the church forward.

The Initiating Leader

How do we lead a congregation into a new, emerging culture? Leading people into change "challenges what people hold dear—their habits, loyalties and ways of thinking—with nothing more to offer perhaps than a possibility."[16] Most people cannot see at the beginning of the change process that the new situation will be any better. They do understand the potential for loss.

The role of the leader in the change process is not always comfortable. Leaders have to provide a number of critical functions. First, it is usually the leaders who have to initiate the change process. If they do not induce the change process, then the discontented people in the congregation will try to induce the change process, thus more likely causing a division in the church or at least creating a win-lose situation. Some of the people in the church who are convinced that we should be entering and becoming immersed into a new, emerging culture are "all but giving up on existing church structures, believing them to be institutionally archaic and out of touch with the demands of today's postmodern emerging culture."[17] While the moderns are looking for stability from the past, the emergents are looking for a radically alternative future. For them it is not about where we have been but about where we might go.

The Shepherding Leader

In addition to leading the change process, leaders must provide the congregation with a psychological safety net as people in the congregation go through this traumatic change. People in the congregation should be reassured that they will be shepherded through this change process. The process will cause people to question their identity and sense of competence. That is a lot to ask of people. They are feeling anxiety and stress in the world outside the church. Now we are asking them to feel that same anxiety within the church. No wonder people resist major change.

Many older people in our church would much rather have a stable present based upon the predictable past than an unstable present based upon an unpredictable future. They feel this uncertain present and future as such a major loss that many people in our churches are turning inward to home schooling, gated communities or "traditional values" in an attempt to fend off the uncertain future.[18] About this time you are asking yourself if the change is worth it. Do you want to be just a manager who creates greater efficiency and says "If it ain't broke, don't fix it"? Or do you sense God calling you to create, not a greater efficiency, but a different environment for the future?

If you believe we are in a new time, an emerging culture, then now might be the best time to shepherd the church into this change process. What if Peter had waited to initiate the change process of the early church? The church would never have left Jerusalem or the surrounding towns. As Peter Senge reminds us, "Learning based on the past suffices when the past is a good guide to the future. But it leaves us blind to profound shifts when whole new forces shaping change arise."[19]

A Worthy Change

As leaders, we have to ask the question, is the gain worth the pain? One author writes, "Although the movement from the old to the new might look and feel chaotic, it represents an opportunity to look at the deeper structures on which the organization has depended. It provides an opportunity to rethink, redirect, reorganize, reposition and rebuild."[20]

In the area of church leadership, we also need to have the foresight to realize that new leadership methods will be necessary in this emerging culture. We cannot just keep on doing leadership the same way. As Albert Einstein said, "No problem can be solved from the same level of thinking that created it."[21] How do we know when the situation requires a new way of leading instead of just working harder? James Osterhaus, a Christian consultant, suggests, "The key question we have to ask ourselves when faced with such a situation is this: 'Can I solve this situation with resources I already have, or does the solution lie in changing people's values, attitudes and habits?' If it is the latter, then we must boldly shoulder the task of producing change."[22]

Change will result when new influences disrupt existing patterns. As we let go of the past and plunge into the uncertainty of the present, new patterns will emerge for the future. When we are faced with significant change, we have to realize that we will not end up in a win-win situation. Win-win solutions, where you do not step on anyone's toes, are not possible.[23] The question one has to ask is, am I willing to put my leadership on the line to lead my congregation or ministry through this change process?

Continuous and Discontinuous Change

We might not be at the edge of a new geographically based culture, but we are in the early stages of a significant cultural paradigm shift. If only we would open our eyes, we would see that we are not crossing a recognizable boundary into a new culture, but rather that this emerging culture is oozing up all around us. We are now rapidly transitioning from a modern Western-dominated culture into an emerging culture that will become more global than Western. As I stated in *Emerging Hope,* "It is vital that we understand as much as we can about this shift because it will affect the way we do ministry in the coming years. In the Western world there have been four major cultural paradigm shifts (transitions) since the death of Christ. The last two transitions have not only impacted the Western world but also have influenced cultures in the Two-Thirds World. Due to increasing globalization, this emerging culture will have even more of an impact throughout the world."[24] As I heard Stan Grenz state many times in conversations, "This shift [from modern to emerging culture] has the potential to be as dramatic as the shift from the Middle Ages to the Renaissance."

Since this cultural shift is so pervasive, we have to let go of our certainty and our current views and be willing to develop a new understanding of what is going on. In this period of transition, existing and emerging leaders need each other. We need the maturity, wisdom and order of the existing leaders, and we need the imagination, creativity and chaos of the emerging leaders. Dee Hock describes this leadership merger as "chaordic leadership."[25]

Existing leaders have to adjust their thinking and not just bring their same systems, structures and ways of doing leadership into the emerging culture. Existing leaders must realize that we cannot rely on the past patterns solely to bring about change. Alan Roxburgh describes the process of looking to the past to bring about change as continuous change. "Continuous change develops out of what has gone before and therefore can be expected, anticipated and managed."[26] The conference at Trinity Evangelical Divinity School was trying to evangelize postmoderns by emphasizing continuous change and using strategies that were appropriate for a modern culture but not for a new culture. Alan Roxburgh describes discontinuous change as "disruptive and unanticipated; it creates situations that challenge our assumptions. . . . Discontinuous change is dominant in periods of history that transform a culture forever, tipping it over into something new."[27]

Let me give you an example of the difference between continuous and discontinuous change. I learned to drive in the United States. Although different parts of the country have their own idiosyncrasies in driving, we all drive on the right side of the road. Driving on the right side of the road is predictable and provides stability. However, if I visited England and decided to drive on the right side of the road because it worked in the past, I would be in for a rude awakening when I realized that everyone else was driving on the left side of the road. I could not drive like I did in the past only better (continuous change). In England I would have to be open to driving completely different. I must be open to discontinuous change.

Forecasting and Foresight

In periods of continuous change we relied upon forecasting. Irene Sanders describes forecasting as follows:

Forecasting is based on analysis of existing conditions and trends. Through analysis and the use of mathematical models, forecasters estimate or calculate a future state. Classical forecasting models are based on the old cause-effect belief that, given a set of initial conditions, all you have to do is project those forward and arrive at a conclusion about the future.[28]

We predict weather through forecasting. We look at thirty-year models of weather patterns to predict where any given weather pattern will head in the next three to seven days for short-range forecasts and thirty days for long-range weather trends. But what happens when the long-term weather pattern is impacted by a major paradigm shift? We are in the midst of just such a shift: global warming. As we are moving into a long-term global warming shift, our forecasting models of the past, based upon continuous change, will no longer prove valid. We will have to develop new understanding and eventually new models.

In times of major paradigm shifts, instead of just *forecasting,* we must also have *foresight.* Sanders describes foresight as "the ability to see what is emerging—to understand the dynamics of the larger context and to recognize new initial conditions as they are forming."[29] In a period of transition we will need some people who can forecast and others who have foresight. In weather prediction we have to have meteorologists who know the old patterns and can see where they are breaking down due to the global-warming paradigm shift. However, we will also have to have other meteorologists who are not tied to the past but can bring the foresight needed to develop new predictive patterns for the future. Both types of meteorologists are important during this time of transition. They need to partner together so we can move forward.

It's necessary to have the same type of partnership in church leadership if we are going to move forward. The church requires both existing and emerging leaders who can work together as we continue transitioning from the modern to the emerging culture. Peter recognized that the church needed to change as it transitioned into the Gentile culture. Peter also recognized that the future leaders of the church would have to come from the Gentile culture. Today we must have the same type of foresight by existing leaders. We will need existing leaders who can recognize that the future leadership of the church will have to come from the emerging leaders. We will need to partner well with the emerging leaders and be willing to give our blessings to this leadership jump.

What are the changes in leadership that need to take place so that this leadership jump occurs smoothly? We will spend the rest of the book looking at the specific leadership jumps that will have to take place as we move from an existing leadership framework to an emerging leadership framework. As we look at the larger jump from existing to emerging leaders, we will look at the following related jumps:

The Leaders' Position

Heroic Leader	→	Post-Heroic Leader
Guarded	→	Vulnerable
Positional Authority	→	Earned Authority

The Leaders' Role

Task	→	Community
Directing	→	Empowering
Destination	→	Journey

Leadership's Future

Aspiring	→	Inspiring

Leadership Jumps

Changes to Consider

1. Set up a process for the existing and emerging leaders in your ministry to discuss how their views of the emerging culture are similar and different.

2. Have a discussion between existing and emerging leaders to see in what areas the church has changed and what areas should still change to minister faithfully and effectively in this emerging culture.

3. Establish a process so emerging leaders can have more of a voice in the future of your church.

4. Together, set up a process for how change can occur in your ministry.

Part Two

THE LEADERS'
POSITION

From Heroic to
Post-Heroic Leadership

Question to ponder:
Why should we move from a heroic to a
post-heroic view of leadership?

As we are moving from a modern culture to a postmodern or emerging culture, we find ourselves in tension with each other. One of those places of tension is how we view leadership. A pastor friend of mine shared with me the struggle his church had just gone through that exemplifies this tension in leadership views that many churches are facing or will soon face. A number of years ago this church had changed from a senior pastor model of leadership to more of a team approach to leadership. This leadership pattern worked well until the church hired a new teaching pastor.

After a period of time, the new teaching pastor felt that the church needed to go back to a senior pastor model where the teaching and leadership role resided in the senior pastor. After much discussion, the rest of the staff, mostly younger, continued to disagree with the plan to return to the old model. But the teaching pastor convinced the elder board to go along with his plan. If they had not gone along with the plan, the teaching pastor would probably have left the church.

When the elders made the change, the majority of the church staff left in the next few months because of the change in the leadership structure of the church. Most of the older people in the church could not understand what the big issue was. Most of the younger leaders were aghast that more people in the church could not understand their perspective. What the church did not fully realize was that they were in the midst of a leadership structure discussion that more and more churches will be having in the coming years. What are the different leadership perspectives between the modern and emerging leaders? What are the biblical models that can guide us in these discussions?

Heroic Modern Leaders

In the modern world, great leaders were characterized in heroic terms. If you asked older existing leaders to name their heroes, they might mention past political leaders like Franklin Roosevelt or Ronald Reagan. They might mention spiritual leaders like Billy Graham or Rick Warren. However, if you asked younger leaders, they might have a harder time thinking of leaders they admire. The political leaders they have known in the early twenty-first century, such as Bill Clinton and George W. Bush, are known more for their weaknesses than for their strengths. They might not be able to think about any spiritual leaders they admire. Actually there are few heroes today. The heroes of the emerging generation tend to be close friends, family members or schoolteachers.

Probably for most of us when we think about leaders, we tend to think about charismatic, larger-than-life figures. As Dan Allender asserts, "When we normally think of a senior pastor, corporate CEO or University president, we think of the top decision maker . . . who makes the final decision. He sits at the top of the pyramid, the place where the buck stops. To most people that's what it means to be a leader."[1] This long-standing philosophy of leadership makes the assumption that leadership rests in individuals who can inspire and influence others to solve the problems, accomplish the task and achieve the goals. Older Americans value John Wayne and Charlton Heston characters in the movies. This view of leadership is rooted in the rugged individualism from the frontier period of our American history. This rugged John Wayne view of leadership is probably a caricature, but it is a caricature that we have accepted.

Many pastors in church leadership today still hold to the great man (rarely the great woman) view of leadership. As Joyce Fletcher states, "The traits commonly associated with traditional, heroic leadership are closely aligned with stereotypical images of masculinity. Men or women can display them, but the traits themselves—such as individualism, assertiveness, and dominance—are socially ascribed to men in our culture."[2] Andy Stanley Jr. describes this view as the follow-me view of leadership. "Follow we never works. It's follow me. God gives a man or a woman the gift of leadership. And any organization that has a point leader with accountability and freedom to use their gift will do well."[3] This view of leadership is known as the heroic leader. The heroic leader is responsible "to determine the direction, to find the right answers, and to carry out the traditional management functions. It's your job to deliver in your area."[4] As we look in the ancient Scriptures, we identify people such as Abraham, Jacob, Moses, Joshua and David as heroic leaders.

The Silo Model of Leadership

Since the church has been immersed in modern culture in the twentieth century, we have created a heroic church-leadership culture that attracts the modern corporate leadership style. So, like the corporate world, the modern church has emphasized a corporate culture where the goals are clear, the mission is clear and there is not a lot of fluff. This type of leadership is goal and program oriented. To move the church forward in this leadership style, the church incorporates a senior pastor and a hierarchical authority leadership model. The buck-stops-here senior leader is the central figure in the church. For the most part, the church will succeed or fail based on the ability of the senior pastor to lead the church in accomplishing the church's mission. This view of leadership became the default view of leadership of the church I mentioned earlier. For many older leaders, this is the only model they know. However, it certainly has its downsides.

This type of leadership model from the Western corporate world tends to induce compliance from its members, not foster commitment or creativity. The stronger the leader, the more people try to comply. When we have a mindset of compliance, we tend to move away from caring for the customers or church members and move toward pleasing the boss. The customer is neglected. In the church all the authority and creativity lies in the senior pastor. In this model the senior pastor is the heroic leader and everyone follows him.

Under the heroic model of leadership, we have a tendency to just hire people for certain positions (senior pastor, young adults pastor, children's ministry director) we want them to have within the church. This leadership style is called the silo model. Each staff person tends to work alone by focusing on his or her sphere of responsibility and following the vision of the senior pastor. In this type of system, each person jockeys for positional power in order to command the resources necessary to accomplish his or her specific part of the plan. Although we do not give these other leaders much of a voice in the direction of the church, we do want them to carry out the vision within their own sphere. In addition, we want them to function in their own sphere without much supervisory or emotional support from the senior leadership. Each member of the church staff functions autonomously from the others. For the independent operator, this is the ideal environment.

The heroic model worked well in a simple, slow-paced industrial world where tasks remained the same and conformity was essential. The small-town world of the mid-twentieth century was an ideal place for this type of leadership. Life changed much more slowly. People's lives also were much simpler. They remained in the same town, usually a factory town. This model has worked well in smaller church communities. However, that pace of life has certainly accelerated over the last few decades.

The Decline of the Heroic Leader

Now more and more people of all ages in the corporate world, and younger leaders in Christian organizations and churches, are beginning to see that the heroic or silo view of leadership is not working as well today as it did ten to twenty years ago. More of the heroic leaders of the past are admitting that the cultural landscape has changed. Some of these leaders are beginning to recognize that the "lone warrior myth of leadership is a sure route to heroic suicide. . . . Nobody is smart enough or fast enough to engage alone the political complexity of an organization or community when it is facing and reacting to adaptive pressure."[5]

With the complexity of today's society, it is no longer assumed that one leader will have all the answers. However, the heroic model of leadership can still have a strong pull. As Jim Collins explains, "The old role is still seductive. Past models have glorified the individual leader, especially when he or she was an entrepreneur. And charismatic style leaders find it hard to let go of the buzz that comes from having an intense, direct personal influence."[6] While in the past power and authority were the necessary characteristics of a leader, today leadership qualities such as character, influence and relational ability are becoming much more important.

The heroic model has a link to Nietzsche's *Übermensch*, the superman. Nietzsche would have approved of the heroic leader, the person who seems invincible. The movies and TV programs of *Superman* were built around Nietzsche's superhero. Nietzsche did not like Jesus. He perceived Jesus to be a weak, not a strong, leader because Jesus did not try to dominate but rather empowered the disciples to lead.

As we move into the emerging culture, people do not trust the heroic leader. We have seen how many heroic leaders fall from the pedestal. Also, with the complexity of today's world, including Christian ministry, the heroic leader is losing effectiveness. We have begun to see that effectiveness depends less on the heroic leader and more on the collaborative efforts of a number of people to create a team environment where together they can move the company, organization or ministry forward. "The hierarchical structures with clearly defined roles are giving way to more horizontal organizations with greater flexibility, [and] room for initiative."[7] Instead of the traditional forms of leadership, leadership models based on teamwork and community are springing up as they seek to bring more people into the leadership core and a decision-making role. This new view of leadership is called post-heroic or shared leadership.

Post-Heroic Leaders of the Future

The post-heroic model of leadership assumes that the role of the leader is not to take sole responsibility (the buck-stops-here mentality), but rather to build a strong team of leaders who share the responsibilities of moving the organization forward. Post-heroic leadership begins with including a larger group of people in the creation and implementation of ideas and with a greater responsibility of making those ideas successful. The result is a shared leadership.

The post-heroic philosophy of leadership is based on a bottom-up transformation fueled by shared power and community building. It releases the potential power of everyone. In the post-heroic leadership model, everyone on the team is a leader. The role of the team leader is to "build a strong team with a common vision and mutual influence, in which members share in the responsibilities of managing."[8] Post-heroic leadership team members also share responsibility for coordination,

> Leadership shares power. It invites rather than coerces. It recognizes rather than manipulates. It engages rather than separates. It serves rather than rules.
>
> **KEVIN FORD**
> *Transforming Church*

providing relief for the constant oversight the heroic leader felt she or he had to provide. Instead of one person trying to control all, all control all.[9]

Early Church Leadership Models

In Scripture we see numerous occasions of post-heroic or shared leadership. The disciples had a shared view of leadership. There was not a hierarchy of leadership among them or a designated leader. In the early church, leadership did not rest on any single person. According to Acts 6, which describes a critical time for the early church, a group of leaders were chosen to serve with no one designated as *the* leader. Leadership was a function shared by a group of people who relied on the Holy Spirit. Later on, the early church leaders formed the Jerusalem Council, which was also a shared leadership model. We see this shared leadership model in place in Acts 15 when Paul and Barnabas were sent by the Antioch church to go to Jerusalem to meet with the leaders of the church, known as the Council of Jerusalem. The council was composed of a whole

> **The story of the church, as depicted in the book of Acts, is one of a community of faith directed by a team of leaders working together toward a common vision. Had the church relied upon a single, incredibly gifted, magnetic individual to replace Jesus, the church would surely have collapsed. What the disciples discovered was that none of them had the complete package of gifts . . . necessary to facilitate the growth of the Christian church, but each had a very significant and defined role to play in that revolutionary undertaking.**
>
> **GEORGE BARNA**
> *The Power of Team Leadership*

group of leaders. James seems to have been the convener of the council, but leadership and decisions were made corporately. This shared leadership model seemed to be pervasive in the early days of the church.

Present Church Leadership Models

Some have suggested that the Trinity is a form of team and offers a shared leadership model. Peter Dickens says, "The Trinity is an extraordinary model of distributed leadership. The concept of heroic leadership invariably suggests a single leader. . . . This [shared leadership model] can only happen when the leaders shift from power to service as their plausibility structure. They must fully embrace not only the concept of service, but intentionally lead from a position that is utterly devoid of power."[10]

Although some of us might miss the John Wayne–type leader, Ken Blanchard exclaims, "You can't (in today's complex culture) make it anymore with just a horse and a couple of guns. . . . None of us are as smart as all of us."[11] While the heroic leadership model can sometimes develop a we-versus-them mentality, the post-heroic leadership model embraces a new style of leadership. Instead of dividing people, it connects them. It emphasizes the we over the I. This shared leadership model develops a group of leaders who possess complementary gifts and skills. They are committed to each other and together lead the organization.

Post-heroic or shared leadership does not mean that there is no leader. All members of the team lead in some capacity based on their gifts. At different times each member of the leadership team can be a leader or a follower. Let me give you a ministry example. In my ministry leadership team, I am the team leader. But if we are discussing spiritual formation or prayer, John Hanna leads us. If missions, Terri Shell is the leader. If multiethnic ministry, Joe Ho and Fred Williams are the leaders. Although I am the overall team leader, in certain areas of discussion, I become a follower instead of a leader because others on the team are more gifted in that area of ministry. Our church, the Chapel Hill Bible Church, has a similar structure of pastors and lay elders. Mark Acuff, one of the pastors, leads us in the vision process. Another pastor, Randy Russell, leads us in spiritual formation. However, if we are talking about leadership development, Roger VanDyke, a lay elder, has been the leader. Keith Newell, another lay elder, has led us in prayer ministry.

Post-heroic leaders do not have all the answers. They understand what they are good at and what their limitations are. Their authority comes less from their formal position and more from their accessibility to their team. As Walt Wright states, "A good team is not a collection of star achievers. It is the star achiever."[12] By that he means that the team takes precedent over any individual.

The church situation I described earlier in the chapter ended up with a power struggle. Basically, that teaching pastor could not see his need for others to share in the leadership. He thought the only way he could lead was by consolidating power rather than distributing it. He saw himself as the hero.

In post-heroic leadership, leaders have to acknowledge and respect their own limitations as well as the gifts God has given each of them in the team. In each of the lists of spiritual gifts in 1 Corinthians, Romans and Ephesians, it is always "some" to be not "one" to be. No one leader has all the gifts required to be a leader. God chooses to give different leaders different gifts so no one leader could just depend on himself or herself but all have to depend on each other and ultimately depend on God. Shared leadership requires giving place to others. Each person leads in his or her area of giftedness. Having many gifted leaders leads to vital ministry and a vital church.

It is time for the church to move away from the myth of the complete leader, the flawless person at the top who's got it all figured out. The sooner leaders stop acting like God, the sooner they will be the leaders God has created them to be. Eddie Gibbs calls the church to "reinstate the team concept of leadership, which embraces the gifts of the many people needed to lead the church into a postmodern and post-Christendom future."[13]

Good to Great Leaders

It is ironic that the corporate world understood the necessity of moving from the heroic leadership model to the post-heroic model long before many churches understood the need. Jim Collins, in his book *Good to Great,* is advocating a post-heroic view of leadership. In Collins's model of leadership, Level 5 leaders first must channel their ego away from themselves and pour all their energy into building a great company. Although these leaders are exceedingly ambitious, they focus their ambition not on themselves but on the company, organization or church.[14]

The good to great leaders know their first responsibility is to bring together the "who" rather than the "what."[15] The initial step is to build a team by getting the right people on the bus. The reason Collins says to start there is this: "If people join the bus primarily because of where it is going what happens if you get ten miles down the road and you need to change direction? You've got a problem. But if people are on the bus because of who else is on the bus, then it's much easier to change directions."[16] While businesses understand the importance of gathering the right team before moving ahead, too often churches in their hiring processes do not take into account the importance of gathering a team that works well together.

Not only do good to great leaders build a team that works well together, but also they try to get the wrong people off the bus. Again, churches and other Christian organizations do not do a good job of helping leaders leave. As we move further into this emerging culture, we should have leaders with a different gift mix than we had five or ten years ago. Instead of the lone-wolf entrepreneur who likes to work alone, we need leaders today who can be team players and together decide who should be on the team and where the team should be going.

Getting the right people on the bus who can work well together as a team allows the organization to move forward with shared leadership. Since in a shared leadership model you have a number of leaders who can lead, it means the "old top-down management structure gives way to flatter, more decentralized forms, and is seen by some experts as a way of promoting agility, proactivity and autonomy."[17]

With more flexibility, a business or ministry can react more quickly to the changing culture. Let me give you an example. The primary strategist for the Eckerd Corporation was Jack Eckerd himself. However, the direction of its competitor Walgreens was developed by a leadership team who through group dialogue came to an agreed-upon direction for the company. As a result, Walgreens has been better able to make the necessary adjustments than Eckerd. As a matter of fact, Eckerd Drug Stores no longer exist. A company that flourished under the heroic leadership model of the twentieth century did not flourish well under the post-heroic twenty-first-century leadership model.

Leadership Team

The CEO or senior-pastor model of leadership will likely have to give way to a team leadership model. This jump will be difficult for many churches. In the post-heroic leadership model, the team leader role is not to take charge but to "design the mechanisms that reinforce and give life to the company's core purpose."[18] The CEO or senior pastor, instead of being the charismatic builder of the organization, becomes the architect welcoming others into the process of building. In the past, too many churches floundered when the senior pastor left. Under a post-heroic leadership model, if the senior pastor leaves, the leadership team does not fall apart.

Thankfully, many churches are moving from the single-leader model to a leadership team based on partnership and giftedness. The role of the pastor is changing from being primarily focused on preaching and pastoral care to being about vision casting and empowering others to do the ministry. This description fits closely with Jesus' style of leadership. To build teams like Jesus did, relationships are the key. For Jesus, teams developed from a shared life.

Walter Wright, in his book *Don't Step on the Rope,* describes this shared life and teamwork by using the analogy of a moun-

---

All along her journey, Dorothy welcomed company. She was glad for a team. By the end of their journey, the lion, the scarecrow, and the tin man have joined Dorothy as peers, partners, friends. Her style of leadership was empowering, ennobling, not patronizing, paternalistic, creating dependency.

BRIAN MCLAREN
"Dorothy on Leadership"

tain climbing team. The shared values of a team determine the success of the team as much as does their shared vision. As Walt admits, "We will not continue to clip onto a rope with people whose decisions we distrust or whose agendas differ from our own. . . . Shared values are the roots of community."[19] These shared values create an environment for the relationships on the team to develop. As those relationships deepen, trust and mutual respect begin to cement the team together. It is this cohesion that creates unity among the members of the team and provides the foundation for the team's effectiveness.

> The leader is not "above" or in any way set apart from the team. Rather, like every member of the team, the leader is a participating, contributing member who just happens to have the assignment of leader for a particular purpose. . . . True teams have a high level of intimacy in relationships of mutual dependence.
>
> **WALTER WRIGHT**
> *Don't Step on the Rope*

Teamwork is not an end in itself but a way of working together to accomplish something that is worth doing. Teams exist to pursue a mission or accomplish a purpose. They draw on these relationships that are developed on the team, and the unity that results from these relationships, to attain a common goal.

Servant Leadership

Leadership on the rope team is all about serving the team. On a rope team, everyone is a leader within his or her sphere of responsibility. Leadership is shared. The appointed leader facilitates the decision-making process. However, the decision resides in the team.

The leader in the post-heroic leadership model must be committed to leading the team. But leading the team calls for not leading from a conquering "come follow me model" but leading from a model of serving and empowering others.

In the Old Testament, when we read the word "king," we tend to think of one with power. However, the word for *king* in the Hebrew means "servant shepherd." The terms *king* and *shepherd* were interchangeable. How different our leadership style might be if we equated king with shepherd. As Dan Allender reminds us, "To be a king meant to shepherd one's people from death to life."[20]

In this emerging culture, we can look to Jesus as our model of a leader. For us as existing leaders, we could do no better than to emulate Jesus' style of leadership. Jesus was not the Teddy Roosevelt "let's storm the hill" type but a shepherd-king type of leader. Jesus, instead of leading by pointing everything to himself, focused on the disciples, his leadership team. Instead of leading with power and control, he focused on serving and empowering the disciples. Jesus, soon before he was going to die on the cross, did not demand that the focus be on his power. Instead Jesus gave up power to serve his disciples.

> Jesus knew that the Father had put all things under his power, and that he had come from God and was returning to God; so he got up from the meal, took off his outer clothing, and wrapped a towel around his waist. After that, he poured water into a basin and began to wash his disciples' feet, drying them with the towel that was wrapped around him. . . .

When he had finished washing their feet, he put on his clothes and returned to his place. ". . . I have set you an example that you should do as I have done for you." (Jn 13:3-5, 12, 15)

How many of our leadership power struggles would go away if we had the attitude of Jesus by becoming a servant leader? If instead of drawing power to ourselves we "washed the feet" of those we led? One of my most memorable times as a leader was when in front of a large Christian gathering I called the people I led to the stage and began washing their feet. It was a simple image of conveying to all gathered there that I saw myself not as the person of power but as a servant leader.

Many New Testament scholars understand Philippians 2:5-11 to be one of the first Christian hymns. If that is the case, then Paul was making a strong statement that like Jesus he viewed himself not as a heroic leader but a post-heroic servant leader. If existing leaders today will willingly give up their power and share it with the emerging leaders, we will then have the possibility of a smooth transition of power from the existing to emerging leaders. As existing leaders, we must not see this move to post-heroic or shared leadership as a fad. As one existing leader has said, "Call it whatever you like: post-heroic leadership, servant leadership. . . . But don't dismiss it as just another touchy-feely flavor of the month. It's real, it's radical and it's challenging the very definition of corporate leadership for the 21st century."[21]

Changes to Consider

1. Explore how your leadership structure can be restructured so that it might be less reliant on one person.

2. Discover the gifts of your leaders to see who should lead the various parts of your leadership team.

3. Establish a process for existing leaders to begin sharing power and authority with emerging leaders.

From Guarded to Vulnerable

Question to ponder:
Why should we as leaders be more vulnerable
with others on our staff team?

I had the distinct privilege of working under the leadership of Gordon MacDonald while he was president of InterVarsity Christian Fellowship. I appreciated his vision for ministry. I learned how to develop as a leader by watching how he led. However, all during the time he was president, neither I nor others got to know Gordon well as a person. Although he would share stories about himself, you could always tell he was measuring what he shared. Gordon was not vulnerable about who he was, his dreams, his fears.

While Gordon was president, he went through a challenging personal crisis. Eventually he stepped down as president. After he left InterVarsity, we kept in touch when I would be in New England or the New York City area. During those times I began to see a different person in Gordon. He was still a formidable leader. But instead of being guarded in personal conversations or in speaking engagements or in his writings, he became more vulnerable. He was willing to share more of himself. And instead of making him a lesser leader, it actually made him a stronger leader.

Perfect Leader

For many of us who are older leaders, we have been taught all our lives to be cautious about what we share with people who work for us. The old wisdom was that if we shared our questions, our pain and our doubts we would not be considered strong leaders. The leaders I knew growing up in the church and in my early years in ministry certainly modeled that cautiousness in sharing their lives. I had many doubts and questions that I never voiced to others because I was taught that it would not be appropriate. I was taught that I had to present an image of having my act together. I know I am not the only leader who was taught that perspective. Spencer Burke, the author of *Making Sense of Church,* shares a similar perspective.

> In seminary, I'd been instructed to not be vulnerable. Under no circumstance were pastors supposed to let their emotions get out of control. Your support system was supposed to be other pastors in the community and people outside of your congregation. You weren't supposed to break down in the pulpit or expose your weak, frail reality.[1]

The business world is no different. In the modern world, business leaders have been taught to project a style of leadership that cries out, "I am in charge! I have all the answers. I can fix all the problems." Above all else, "I am in control." To portray this image, the leaders need to project calm and self-assurance to people around them.[2] They can never or rarely let others who are on their leadership team know when they have doubts.

This type of leadership style rubs off on the emerging leaders. They initially feel that they have to appear to have their act together in front of the existing leaders. This type of bulletproof mentality will cause the younger leaders to "put on masks of invincibility instead of placing greater value on authenticity."[3] Instead of asking for help from the older leaders, they will pretend to have all the answers.

The result of this type of leadership model is that the leader and others on the team are isolated from each other. The leader pushes any doubts below the surface and does not deal with them. Too often this action bubbles up in other ways. It is not surprising to me that many of the leaders who have extramarital affairs or who emotionally or physically abuse their spouse or children are people who are guarded about sharing their struggles or doubts with other people.

Thankfully, some leaders who feel like they have to be guarded with people on their own leadership team do find other outlets to share their doubts. In my thirty years in ministry I have found myself at different times being a confidant for pastors or other ministry leaders in my community. I was a safe person. Although I was primarily in campus and not church ministry, I understood the feelings they were having or the issues they were dealing with in their churches or in their marriages. I got to see them in a vulnerable place.

However, I know that their colleagues in their church or ministry did not see this side of them. How did this guardedness affect the way they related to their team members or the way their team members related to them? How did it impact the way they related to the people in their congregation? Brad Bell, who is now a pastor himself, recalls how he was affected by his pastor, who portrayed the perfect life. "In my experience in a traditional church, I never knew my pastor sinned because he never gave us a glimpse of any struggle in his life. My conclusion was self-doubt and self-condemnation. What the heck is wrong with me? Why can't I be like my pastor?"[4] Because Brad's pastor never became vulnerable in front of Brad or anyone else in the congregation, no one in the congregation fully developed trust in the pastor.

Trust-Building Leader

Patrick Lencioni relates a story of how a company faltered because the CEO failed to build trust among his team. In a study looking into why the company collapsed, it was discovered that one of the major contributing factors was the leader's inability to model vulnerability that developed an atmosphere of trust. As one executive reported to Lencioni, 'No one in the team was ever allowed to be smarter than him in any area because he was the CEO.' As a result, team members would not open up to one another and admit their own weaknesses or mistakes."[5]

In any ongoing team I am leading, I make it a point to create an environment for people to share themselves through sharing their life story, sharing their emotions and sharing what is happening in their lives. Sometimes this sharing takes place in formal meetings, but it also happens in informal gatherings.

One of my former staff talked about the importance of creating memories together. I remember how one of the closest elder boards I served on became close because we took the time to go on camping trips together. A number of years ago I would take my InterVarsity leadership team and their families to the beach each summer. Over the week we became very close—as well as accomplished all the business we needed to accomplish. How do the teams you lead or are a member of develop vulnerability?

Paul's Example

Paul is an example of a leader who was willing to be vulnerable with the people he led. As he shared with the Corinthian church,

> In order to keep me from becoming conceited, I was given a thorn in my flesh, a messenger of Satan, to torment me. Three times I pleaded with the Lord to take it away from me. But he said to me, "My grace is sufficient for you, for my power is made perfect in weakness." Therefore I will boast all the more gladly about my weaknesses, so that Christ's power may rest on me. That is why, for Christ's sake, I delight in weaknesses, in insults, in hardships, in persecutions, in difficulties. For when I am weak, then I am strong. (2 Cor 12:7-10)

Paul always led through his humility and his vulnerability. He saw his power as originating, not through his own strength, but rather in his weakness, which was made strong through Christ's power. More of our leaders today should follow Paul's example of being willing to admit weaknesses so they can rest in Christ's strength. An attitude of vulnerability will both be freeing to the leader and give more freedom to the people they lead to admit weaknesses. The result will be a lot more freedom for people to be themselves.

Too many leaders pay little attention to understanding their own emotional needs and therefore are not prepared to help others on the team deal with their own emotions. As we think about hiring or developing people for our staff team, we consider their intellectual capability, their theological acuity and their administrative ability. However, we rarely think about their emotional intelligence. Emotional intelligence is one's ability to empathize, to feel another's pain. Especially in times of organizational transitions, everyone feels a sense of loss or fear, has reservations about the new directions and needs to deal with these emotions. If the leaders cannot share their own feelings, they will not foster an environment where others can be open. The result is that everyone is left on their own to deal with the changes.

As I said earlier, many existing leaders have been taught that it is not wise to be close friends with people they lead. I have a couple of people in ministry who I admire immensely and who have that commitment. They will take the time to hear how people are doing, but they are committed to keeping an emotional distance between themselves and the people they lead. Maybe that view of ministry worked in a modern culture. However, in this emerging culture, it is imperative that we lead not just with our mind but also with our heart. Emotional intelligence is just as important as other leadership traits. The people we lead need to see us for who we are. We have to invite them into our homes and share our own lives so they feel free to share about their lives.

> Conventional management wisdom has taught us for decades that keeping one's distance from others, especially those one leads, is essential to good leadership. To be objective, one mustn't get too close. By keeping that distance, the leader would ensure that her ability to make decisions . . . would never be compromised.
>
> **RON CARUCCI**
> *Leadership Divided*

Vulnerable Leader

Each year I meet for three days with all of the new InterVarsity staff in our region. We usually have ten to fifteen staff in those meetings. My wife, Betsy, and I host these meetings in our home so these first-year staff can get to know us as real people. In the past, when the numbers were smaller, many of these staff have stayed in our home. We still have all the meals in our home. Hopefully, they see me not just as the thirty-year veteran regional director but as a real person. This meeting takes place in February when they have to decide whether they want to remain on staff now that their internship is coming to an end. The regional leadership team that I lead will also be deciding whether we think they should remain on staff for the next three years.

It is a time of great anxiety on their part. Many emotions are flooding through them. Instead of ignoring those emotions, we take time to deal with them. I stumbled onto an exercise we now go through every year. I ask each of them to sit in the interview chair in our house. It used to be pink but has since been recovered in red. But people still call it the pink chair. Now, you have to know that, almost to the week one year before, each of them sat in this same chair to be interviewed for staff by me and the regional leadership team. We try to make the interview as relaxed as possible, so we hold it in my house. We also want all the candidates to have a similar experience, so we have each of them sit in this same chair for the interview. Now, one year later, I am having each of them again sit in this "pink chair." I ask them two questions. How did you feel about the interview, and what has God taught you about yourself during this first year on staff? Then after that person shares, all the other first-year staff can ask them any questions about the interview or their first year on staff.

To set the tone, I sit in the chair first and share about my hiring process and my first year on staff in 1975. I share with the others that, although we did not know it at the time, we got letter grades on our staff application. I stumbled onto my personnel file a couple of years later when I became InterVarsity's area director. My application had a C+ on the top of the first page with the comment "Never could work at a Johns Hopkins type school." I also share with these first-year staff that my sole vision during my first year on staff at UNC Chapel Hill was that I did not want to be known as the staff worker who killed one of InterVarsity's largest chapters. They then have a chance to pepper me with questions about my first year on staff.

I do that exercise to help them see me as a person who was probably more scared during my first year than any of them are. I also share with them my continuing doubts and questions. The result is that I have created an environment where these staff, who are younger than my own children, can be vulnerable with me and each other because I have been vulnerable with them. The rest of the evening I just sit back in amazement as they share their first-year staff stories openly with each other and with me.

The example I set at these gatherings has continued to allow these staff to be vulnerable with me during the rest of their time on staff. I put this relational vulnerability to the test more than a year ago. Immediately after hearing about the Virginia Tech massacre in April 2007, my thoughts turned to our staff at that school. After making sure they had all the resources they needed for the coming days, I told the two staff working with undergraduate students that I wanted my role with them to be one where we just talked about how they personally were dealing with the tragedy. I spent much time on the phone in the coming days listening to how they were doing. I said I wanted to be the person they could yell at, cry with or just talk with. I think I was able to serve the staff in this way because I had already established a relationship with them in their first year and in succeeding years on staff where we were vulnerable with each other.

Emerging leaders are crying out for an environment where the existing leaders and they can develop trust through vulnerability. We are coming to see that leaders in the business or religious world who know their strengths and weaknesses, and are willing to appropriately share them with their team, tend to be far more capable and effective leaders. Ron Carucci wonders, "Why does the notion of being accessible and close to others cause many leaders fear? Because many leaders still have yet to learn that the exposure of their humanity and even their failures buys them *more* credibility, not less."[6] Older leaders have to be willing to continue to learn and transition in this changing world. Kerry Bunker describes what happens to leaders who are unwilling to change.

> They fall into the trap of trying to lead an organization in an evolving world without actually evolving themselves. They make decisions based on old knowledge, assumptions and habits. They fall into a rut and wind up repeating past mistakes. . . . If the leader stops growing then the organization stops growing as well.[7]

Our understanding of leadership, both in the business world and the religious world, is certainly changing. Scott Rodin, former president of Eastern Seminary, shares the story that if he were asked ten years ago what Scripture epitomized his leadership ideal, he would have gone to Nathan's command to King David: "Whatever you have in mind, go ahead and do it, for the LORD is with you" (2 Sam 7:3). He goes on to say that today, if he were asked that same question, he would have a very different answer. He would go to the apostle Paul speaking about Jesus' incarnation: "He made himself nothing by taking the very nature of a servant" (Phil 2:7). Rodin's point is that in Jesus we see that the trappings of leadership were dismissed.[8] Instead of coming with power and control, Jesus came with humility and vulnerability. We see Jesus not as CEO of a Fortune 500 company but as our model for leadership in this emerging culture. We have to be leaders who are humble, recognizing that we are not perfect, and be able to create an ethos where those around us feel comfortable taking risks and making mistakes.

Won't that type of openness show our weaknesses? Won't we lose our legitimacy to lead because we come across as weak? We should bury the idea that we need to be perfect, or at least guarded with what we share, in order to be a good leader. As one leader has acknowledged, "Facing our imperfections frees us to live in the grace our God has called us to and, in so doing we invite others into that same relationship with our God."[9] Many of us who are existing leaders should heed the call that the Word of God must be first a word *to* the pastor in order for it be heard as a word *through* the pastor. If we expect others to be vulnerable with us, we must first be vulnerable with ourselves.

Rob Goffee and Gareth Jones, in their book *Why Should Anyone Be Led by You?* proclaim the necessity of vulnerability: "Clearly, demonstrating strengths lends leaders legitimacy—but not if weaknesses are denied. The desire to be led by a real person demands that we know something of a leader's human foibles and shortcomings. The claim of perfection will rarely convince us of another's humanity."[10] That was the modern model of leadership.

In the emerging culture model of leadership, sharing our weaknesses as well as our strengths actually lends more legitimacy to our leadership. As one emerging leader exclaims, "People are sick of packaged, easy answers. They want to hear pastors who have as many questions as they have answers."[11] Emerging leaders want to see the real person, not the false image existing leaders sometimes project. Growing up in a world where they have seen parents and societal and church leaders continually fail (and being so aware of their own failures), emerging leaders need existing leaders who are willing to admit their own weaknesses. Emerging leaders can identify and relate to existing leaders who show their own vulnerability. Instead of being a liability, vulnerability is a hallmark of leadership in the emerging culture. By the existing leader being willing to be vulnerable, the emerging leaders feel like they have been given permission to be vulnerable.

Approachable Leader

In the business and religious worlds, people today are looking for leaders who are also "approachable, touchable, transparent and real . . . not someone who periodically comes down from the mountain to deliver a prescription for life or platitudes of hype."[12] Part of that approachability comes from leaders admitting when they have made mistakes and asking for forgiveness.

I am sure there are many things my wife and I did wrong in raising our children. However, I know one thing we did right. Even when our children were very young, if we did something wrong, such as raise our voice with them or forget to do something we said we would do, we asked for their forgiveness. I do not know how many times I had to ask for their forgiveness during those more than twenty years they were in our house. I lost track long ago. But that simple step of asking forgiveness led to an approachability and transparency that still exist in our relationships. While growing up, our children would share things they did wrong and ask for our forgiveness because they saw us practicing the same thing with them. I know our children were more vulnerable with us than many of their friends were with their parents. Some of our friends said they were glad that they did not know a lot of the things their children did while growing up. I am so glad I did, because our relationship was built on trust and approachability. Even though our children have long since stopped living with us, we still have an approachable relationship. As existing leaders, we should have the same type of approachability with the team we lead. Having others hear us say "I'm sorry" or "I am wrong" helps to take us off the pedestal and places us on the ground alongside the others on our team.

Authentic Leader

A few years ago Brian McLaren put forth a new model for leadership, one most people would not have dreamed to consider: Dorothy from *The Wizard of Oz*.

> At first glance, Dorothy is all wrong as a model of leadership. She is the wrong gender (female) and the wrong age (young). Rather than being a person with all the answers, who knows what's up and where to go and what's what, she is herself lost, a seeker, often bewildered, and vulnerable. These characteristics would disqualify her from modern leadership. But they seem to be her best credentials for postmodern leadership.[13]

One of the critical characteristics we see in Dorothy is that she admits when she does not know the answers to all the questions. She admits she does not know even the direction they should be going.

Like Dorothy in *The Wizard of Oz,* we as leaders can admit when we do not know all the answers. Since we are all on this uncharted journey together into this emerging culture, what we need most from our leaders is honesty. Think about it. Who do you turn to when you have fears and disappointments? Is it the person who portrays the image that he has all the answers? Or is it the person who say that she is still learning? It is the one who admits to not knowing all the answers but believes that God will help all of us find the way we should be going. We trust that person because she is more real, more genuine. We can relate with her more easily.

Sometimes we have to change the whole leadership culture to become more vulnerable and authentic. John Burke and the church leadership team at Gateway in Austin, Texas, have tried to change the whole church from the start. "From the very first service at Gateway, we've had a motto: No perfect people allowed. We find ways to say No perfect people allowed over and over again."[14]

As all of us, starting with the leaders, become more open about our strengths and weaknesses, the whole church becomes more honest. The overall impact is a church or organization that dwells in a climate of authentic relationships. These relationships, built on integrity, trust and honesty, become more like a covenant. In a covenantal relationship, others are treated with care and respect. When people experience covenantal relationships, they feel valued and safe. The organizational culture becomes a caring, authentic community.

The Learning Leader

Randall White suggests the concept of the "child leader." At first glance this concept is the polar opposite of all our modern concepts of leadership. In the modern world, leaders are bigger than life, strong and all knowing. These skills are poorly matched in a world of uncertainty.[15] Instead of portraying an attitude of all-knowingness, we should portray an attitude of learning. We have to enter into a

---

- What would happen if we treated each other with honesty and respect?

- What would happen if we could trust and believe in the genuineness of our position as leaders?

- What would happen if we believed our leaders were not operating from self-interest?

- What would happen if we began to laugh from our mistakes and learn from them?

- What would happen if leaders were candid about what was happening, instead of spinning information for the best effect?

KATHLEEN ALLEN
"Authenticity"

---

period of discovery. Children are discovering all the time.

As I write this chapter, our grandson Asher is discovering how to walk. He will struggle to stand, then proceed across the room with glee, excited about his new world of walking. His learning to walk puts him in a vulnerable state. He is learning how to balance himself, learning how to stop, learning how to move from carpet to wood floor. He falls down fifty times each day. He gets frustrated and will share his frustration with everyone around him. However, he has developed a spirit of learning

Asher could have decided to continue to crawl. He had mastered that skill. He was self-assured and competent in crawling. However, he was willing to become vulnerable again with himself and everyone around him so he could discover a new world called walking. He was willing to place himself in a situation where he needed others to help him discover and learn this new world of walking. Like Asher, Dorothy was willing to lead herself, and the others following her, into discovering a new world. To lead in this kind of new discovery, we have to admit, "We are not in Kansas anymore!" Dorothy had to be vulnerable with others around her and to be in a learning mode.

We are all in a learning mode in this emerging culture. In today's culture one of the most important statements a leader can make is "I don't know." That little statement will free us all to see we are on this journey together into this emerging culture. It will free the existing leaders to not put on a façade of competency but instead have an attitude of learning. When the existing leaders can admit their vulnerability, the emerging leaders will be much more open to share their inadequacies.

As I shared earlier in this chapter, I admired Gordon MacDonald's leadership gifts. He led boldly. However, even Gordon admits that we all should be learners today. In a recent article titled "Who Stole My Church?" Gordon declares, "There may be new ways to evangelize and to do church. The old way is becoming obsolete and ineffective."[16] Gordon, like all of us, has to relearn how to minister and lead in the emerging culture. Together we can move forward, neither group having to pretend they have their act together, but knowing they need each other.

Spending Time Together

How does a team of existing and emerging leaders develop this type of vulnerability that is so crucial for a leadership team to move forward in this new culture? The first step is spending time together as a team in a variety of venues. For many existing leaders, when they think of spending time together, they think of formal staff meetings. Don't get me wrong. Those meeting have their place. I was recently leading a teaching team of staff who were preparing to teach a week-long course for about fifty InterVarsity staff from all over the country. The teaching team was also from all over the country. I was committed to not make the same mistake that I thought we made the previous year when we did not take any time to get to know each other on the teaching team.

So during the first meeting of this teaching team of six staff, I took close to two hours of our time to listen to each of us share our stories. As we hear our stories, we become more relaxed around each other and much more committed to developing a team that works well together. I did not have any expectation that we would develop into a close community in a week of working together. However, I did see that taking the time to get to know each other built closeness in the team that was not there a year ago when we did not take the time to get to know each other. During the week, I saw the teaching team spend time caring for each other and wanting to get to know each other in a deeper way. I am convinced the closeness of the team had its origin in the time we took in the beginning to get to know each other.

During the various years when I have been chair of our church's board of elders, I have always taken the time for us to share about our lives and pray for each other. We have also had outings and retreats where we created memories and got to know each other. And it was because we took the time to be together that we were able to work through the hard issues that faced us. The time we spent building a bond with each other was well worth it. We actually got more accomplished in our meetings together because we had developed a bond or unity with each other.

For many emerging leaders, formal meetings are not the primary place to build vulnerability and trust. It is during the breaks or after the official meeting is concluded or while eating meals together that vulnerability and trust are developed. Let me give you an example. I was invited as one of the elders into my church's staff meeting where one of the pastors and I shared opposing views of whether women can be elders and pastors in our church. The meeting, which lasted ninety minutes, was fruitful. However, the real discussions happened after the meeting in groups of two or three staff where the younger staff shared how they really felt about the discussion.

Although I was on my way out the door, I stayed to enter into two of the informal discussions. It was in those informal discussions that the younger staff were willing to be vulnerable and I was able to be more vulnerable. From many existing leaders' perspectives, the meeting concluded at the end of the formal meeting. From the younger, emerging leaders' perspectives, the real meeting was just beginning at the end of the formal meeting. Vulnerability and trust more readily develop during the informal gatherings of staff. It is in the informal gatherings where the power dynamic lessens. It is in the informal gatherings where trust and authenticity begin to develop. It is in the informal times where most of us can be more real.

For many men, and for a growing number of women, it is also the shared experience or sports activity that creates an environment for vulnerability and trust to develop. I am sure there is some deep psychological reason why this is true. However, I do not know what that reason is. I just know it is true. When my son was in his teens, I tried my hardest to ask him questions so he would open up to me. I know all the tricks about asking open-ended versus closed questions. However, nothing seemed to work until I realized that the best way to get him to open up was to watch a Red Sox baseball game on TV or play a round of Frisbee golf together. Inevitably it was in those times of doing things together and creating a shared bond that Andrew and I had our best conversations. What do you do for fun with your leadership team? What memories have you created together? It is in those times of shared experiences that vulnerability and trust are developed and authenticity is the result.

Caring for Each Other

Why are vulnerability and authenticity so important for the emerging leaders? Many of the young emerging leaders of the church or secular world have few models of people who have really cared for them. For many of them, their parents have been too busy either building their own careers or focusing on their own pleasures, which too often has led to divorce.

Out of the forty InterVarsity staff in my region who are under the age of thirty, about half of them come from homes with divorced parents or from highly dysfunctional family situations. As I read the sixteen applications of the staff candi-

> Within this climate of suspicion, postmoderns above everything else want to experience authenticity. They are interested not so much in our truth claims as in the extent to which our lives correspond to the truth we proclaim.
>
> **EDDIE GIBBS**
> *LeadershipNext*

dates who interviewed last week in the pink chair at our house, I wept on numerous occasions as they shared about their family situations and dysfunctional relationships. These are the future leaders of the church.

As the adage goes, leaders should not only "talk the talk" but also "walk the walk." Although it took him a number of years to make the change, Robert Lewis of Fellowship Bible Church in Little Rock realized that the church culture does not reside in buildings or programs but in people who do not merely talk about an idea but embody it.[17] The emerging leaders are looking for authenticity. They are looking for leaders who demonstrate a consistency between words and deeds. In other words, they do what they preach. Whereas modern, existing church leaders were valued for their knowledge and sermons, postmodern, emerging leaders will be more valued for their character and example. Who we are will matter much more than what we do.

Although I do not think we are meaning to send this signal, too often as existing leaders we communicate that we care much more about what a leader does than about who a leader is. We are concerned more about competency than character. We are still looking at leadership through a modern culture lens instead of through an emerging culture lens. It is easy for us to slip into a modern view of leadership. However, it is critical in this emerging culture to develop a posture of leadership that emphasizes relationships, vulnerability and trust. Who we are in relationship with one another on the leadership team becomes the foundation for the success of our leadership team and the success of our church or organization.

As we become vulnerable, we develop trust with others on our leadership team. Being vulnerable also helps to create an environment where others on the team will feel safe to be vulnerable. Providing hospitality within that safe environment establishes not only a safe place but also a place where healing of our brokenness can take place. Although what I have just described is not the usual model for leadership in the world or the church, Dan Allender among others thinks it should be. "God calls us to brokenness, not performance; to relationships, not commotion; to grace, not success."[18] As we will see in the next couple of chapters, if we existing leaders are willing to give up our positions of power and authority and become more vulnerable and hospitable, we will have earned much more authority or influence than we ever could ever imagine.

Changes to Consider

1. What steps can you take to become more of an approachable leader?

2. How can you develop a team environment where vulnerability is an essential component of your leadership team?

3. What can you do to develop a whole church that is characterized by authentic relationships?

4. What are specific ways you can spend more time together as a leadership team getting to know each other?

From Positional Authority
to Earned Authority

Question to ponder:
Why is the hierarchical view of leadership in decline?

At one of the emerging cultures seminars I led in the Southwest, I had the opportunity to get to know two pastors from the same church. It was obvious early on in my separate conversations with each of them that they had very different perspectives on their working relationship. George, the senior pastor, was proud that his church was on the "cutting edge" of ministry to the emerging culture. He was pleased with himself that his church was willing to bring on Tom, an emerging leader, as minister in their alternative worship service. George thought that Tom and he had a great relationship.

As I began to talk separately with Tom, I got a different picture. Tom was thankful that George and the church had taken the risk to start a ministry to the emerging culture in their city. However, Tom felt constrained by what he was allowed and not allowed to do. George made it clear that he, George, was in charge. He also let Tom know that, whenever Tom wanted to do anything, he was to run it by George and the elders of the church.

From Tom's perspective, George started their relationship by using his position of power to let Tom know who was in charge. He let Tom know where Tom fit into the leadership structure of the church. George acted like he did not fully trust Tom. Tom wanted to build a relationship with George. He wanted to let George know he was not always sure of what direction this new ministry should be taking. However, when he tried to share his uncertainty with George, George took it as a sign of weakness on Tom's part. George began telling Tom what he should be doing in reaching out to the emerging culture.

Although Tom realized that he did not always know what to do, George did not have a clue of how to reach out to the emerging culture. The result: George was excited about what was happening, while Tom was becoming more disillusioned about not only the future of the ministry but also his relationship with George. How had they gotten to this point? To answer this question, we will have to look at how authority is viewed by existing and emerging leaders.

The Decline of the Hierarchical Leader

One fallout from postmodernism is the fact that the dominant Western worldview in today's culture is skepticism toward all types of hierarchical authority. There are many reasons for this change, from the breakdown of the family to the questioning of truth claims. I mentioned in chapter three that where we once held heroes in high esteem, we now have few heroes outside the sports arena. Within the space of one generation, the word *boss* has changed from a positive designation of authority to a negative term that refers to one who is distant from others.[1]

So, how do we view leadership in this emerging culture? The

role of the leader is certainly changing. Gone are the days when the position of the leader meant that whatever the leader says goes because that person is "in charge." There is now a link between one's attitudes toward positional authority and how people prefer to be led. For people who have an aversion to formal authority and to a command-and-control type of leader, they will show little tolerance or respect for domineering supervisors or senior pastors. They will either rebel against or depart from this type of leader. Furthermore, their motivation will plummet under this type of hierarchical leader. One may obey the leader who leads with power and positional authority, but one will not be motivated to serve under that leader, due to a lack of respect.

During the 1980s, InterVarsity Christian Fellowship went through a major upheaval surrounding our national leadership. Jim McLeish, the president of InterVarsity at the

> [Today,] the word "authority" inspires only suspicion and revolt. . . . What does it really mean to be in charge of anything? Nothing. Because in the new and increasingly flattened world, being in charge is an illusion. Being in charge only worked (and marginally so) in a world of slow change; in a predictable universe where information (and thus, power) is ensconced in the hands of a few. But that world is gone.
>
> SALLY MORGENTHALER
> "Leadership in a Flattened World"

time, assumed that because he had the position of the president all of us needed to be loyal to him. He led from a position of power. It led to a major leadership crisis in the organization.

Although we did not fully realize it at the time, some of us were beginning to say that positional authority was less important than earned authority. Jim had the position of leader. However, by his actions, he had not earned his authority in the eyes of many staff in the organization.

A Clash of Leadership Values

I am beginning to see that more and more organizations are having the same clash that InterVarsity had twenty years ago. It is a clash between two views of leadership, one existing and one emerging. One demands loyalty based upon position. The other gives respect based upon earning it. We are now in the midst of a structural change in the way people are responding to positional leadership. George and Tom certainly have different views. George thinks it is obvious that Tom would welcome his instructions because George is the person in charge. However, Tom does not feel that George has fully earned his respect.

Gone are the days of the General Patton–type of leader who led by fear. General Patton made the statement "I do not care if my men stop being afraid of the Germans, but, by God, they had better not stop being afraid of me." That older era was also the one that coined the phrase "organization man," describing a person who was loyal to a company.[2] So loyalty to either the leader or the organization was a key element of modern leadership.

In the past, authority was often identified with rigid and tightly managed hierarchical boundaries. It became confused with dominance. However, the trend today is toward flatter organizations with more flexible boundaries. Differences among titles, positions and roles have become deemphasized. Getting work done often requires more collaboration among superiors, subordinates and peers. Recognizing who is in charge becomes less important than getting the job done.

In many corporations and churches, the people who have the least positional authority but the most earned authority are the administrative assistants. They might not be in charge, but they get the job done. We should recognize people on our teams who get the job done. Behind the scenes with a humble heart, administrative assistants or volunteers on our teams are earning respect and authority even though they do not occupy positions of authority.

John Stott, in *Basic Christian Leadership,* reminds us that Christian leadership should be marked by humility and service, not position and power. Church leaders are to be shepherds of God's people, not greedy for money, but eager to serve. They are not to lord it over those entrusted to them.[3]

> You know that those who are regarded as rulers of the Gentiles lord it over them, and their high officials exercise authority over them. Not so with you. Instead, whoever wants to become great among you must be your servant, and whoever wants to be first must be slave of all. For even the Son of Man did not come to be served, but to serve, and to give his life as a ransom for many.
>
> **MARK 10:42-45**

At no point does Christianity come into more violent confrontation with the secular mindset than when it comes to an insistence on humility, with all the weakness it entails. The world values power, not humility. According to John Stott, "We have drunk in more of the power philosophy of Friedrich Nietzsche than we realize."[4] While most American forms of leadership are based on the cultural norm that leadership equals power, the Bible contains clear warnings about the use and abuse of power. In the Old Testament, we see how the pride of King Uzziah led to his downfall (2 Chron 26:15-16). In the New Testament, we read how Jesus warned the apostles against using their authority and leadership as the leaders did in secular society. The Christian leaders needed in the world today are those who know that God's power will be exhibited, not by the leaders' display of power, but in their display of weakness.

Churches that are based on a senior pastor model that gives complete authority and power to the senior pastor, and organizations that are based on a strict hierarchical view of leadership, are going to be in crisis as we move further into this emerging culture. These cultural changes will play a pivotal role in shaping how leadership is viewed in the future. Jay Conger, in an article in the *Organization of the Future,* proclaims, "These generational transitions are like a riptide; their force is not completely visible on the surface. . . . If, as managers of the organization of the future, we do not understand these dynamic forces, we are likely to be tumbled in their surf."[5]

The role of the leader is changing. Gone are the days when the norm or even the preferred role of the leader is one of command and control. Emerging leaders no longer have an unquestioned respect for existing leaders. The never-ending scandals that have plagued leaders in all fields, from corporate to political to religious institutions, have reinforced the idea among young leaders that all leaders are human and do not belong on pedestals.

How can we change the way we do leadership in this new environment? If you are an emerging leader, you will be encouraged to realize that most of the existing leaders know they need to change. They know the ways they were taught to lead are no longer as valid as they once were.

> **I know there are many thousands in leadership positions who know they are failing their people and desperately desire help in developing effective leadership skills. Many have long ago recognized that the old ways of leading through command-and-control and barking orders are largely ineffective when working with a diverse workplace . . . the vast majority of whom do not trust power people.**
>
> **JAMES HUNTER**
> *The World's Most Powerful Leadership Principle*

Earning Respect

Leadership in the future will be based more on being than on doing. In the past, it was assumed that power lies within the position. However, today the character of the person in the position is valued more than the position itself. This requires the leader to live by the values and vision of the organization. Actually, the performance of the leader and the organization will flow from who they are as much as what they do.

Leaders will have to be authentic people who are respected. However, as Christine Zust states, "The only way to command respect from others is *not* to demand it. Leaders who are admired and respected have *earned* that admiration and respect. Respect is given to others only when they are deemed worthy of receiving the honor."[6] The only respect or authority deserving of people's allegiance today is freely given by those being led because they see the leader is one who is willing to be vulnerable (as we saw in the last chapter) and act as a servant.[7]

Many people did not know that going into the recent Super Bowl season of the New York Giants, Tom Coughlin, the coach of the New York Giants, and many of the Giants players were at odds with each other. At the beginning of the year, Coach Coughlin was viewed as the enemy by many of his players. Mark Maske, a *Washington Post* writer, described the upcoming year as follows:

> It was a make-or-break season for the coach who has been known for his taskmaster ways, from his lengthy list of meticulous rules (which at one time in his career reportedly included no slouching during team meetings and no kneeling during practices) to his disdain of players getting hurt to his punishments for showing up merely on time for a meeting instead of the required five minutes early.[8]

During the Super Bowl season, Coach Coughlin became softer around the edges. He began to relate to his players on a more personal basis. He moved from leading from a place of positional authority to earning the respect of his players as he related to them in a more personal way. As one of the Giants wide receivers stated, "I think he has made more of an effort, and I think him making an effort was enough to win over most of the players."[9] As Tom Coughlin led more from an earned authority position, his players were more willing to follow his leadership. The result was that they won the Super Bowl. Coach Coughlin was willing to change. Are we willing to change how we lead?

A great biblical example of this type of earned authority appears
in the story of Barnabas. In the early church, Barnabas was one of
the few existing leaders who realized that if the church was going
to expand it would require a new type of leader. So Barnabas, when
he heard about Paul's conversion, sought Paul out to develop a ministering relationship with him. Barnabas introduced Paul to other
leaders and began to take Paul on ministry trips with him.

However, Barnabas was not only in a teaching relationship with
Paul; he was also in a learning posture with this emerging leader.
Barnabas realized that Paul had new ideas about how to expand the
ministry. As Barnabas brought Paul into a relationship with himself
and was willing to learn from Paul, Paul's respect for Barnabas
grew. Barnabas had earned, not demanded, authority over Paul.

Eventually Paul took on the role of the main leader. The references in the book of Acts change from "Barnabas and Paul" to
"Paul and Barnabas." Barnabas grew in his realization that Paul,
not himself, was the person God had gifted to move the church
forward. Barnabas was willing to let his authority diminish and
Paul's increase. It was the influence that Barnabas had on Paul that
gave him authority. And it was finally the willingness of Barnabas
to switch leadership positions with Paul that allowed the mission of
the church to go ahead.

Emerging leaders can learn from existing leaders. Existing
leaders need to be willing to eventually give over authority and
leadership to emerging leaders who will be the leaders to move
us forward in ministry within this emerging culture. The existing
leaders move from a position of power, where they are in control,
to a position of empowerment and servanthood, where they encourage the emerging leaders to lead.

In the story I shared in the beginning of this chapter, George had yet to learn how to change his relationship with Tom from one who was in charge to one who was mentoring Tom as well as learning from Tom. George was leading from a position of power instead of a position of servanthood.

Compassionate Leadership

As Max De Pree suggests, "The first responsibility of a leader is to define reality. The last is to say thank you. In between the two, the leader must become a servant."[10] Scott Rodin writes, "Godly leadership is a call to a lifestyle of an ever-decreasing thirst for authority, power and influence, where the quest for reputation is replaced by the power of God's anointing."[11] De Pree goes on to say that leaders are called to become "abandoned to the needs of the followers." Some of those needs include compassion and fairness. Younger leaders also need people who are willing to be held accountable themselves and "who does not fear truth—seeing it, accepting it, and telling it."[12]

One of the things emerging leaders want to see from older leaders is not only that they will be willing to be vulnerable with them but also that they will be more willing to care for the emerging leaders. The emerging leaders, as they "struggle to come to terms with their own brokenness, their disillusionment with authority, the dysfunctionality of their home experience, . . . stand more than ever in need of the kind of leaders more attuned to washing feet than making speeches."[13] Jesus, on the night before he was arrested, his last night with the disciples, chose to begin the evening with them, not by showing them his power or his competence, but by caring for them through washing their feet.

It was just before the Passover Festival. Jesus knew that the hour had come for him to leave this world and go to the Father. Having loved his own who were in the world, he loved them to the end.

The evening meal was in progress, and the devil had already prompted Judas, the son of Simon Iscariot, to betray Jesus. Jesus knew that the Father had put all things under his power, and that he had come from God and was returning to God; so he got up from the meal, took off his outer clothing, and wrapped a towel around his waist. After that, he poured water into a basin and began to wash his disciples' feet, drying them with the towel that was wrapped around him. . . .

When he had finished washing their feet, he put on his clothes and returned to his place. "Do you understand what I have done for you?" he asked them. "You call me 'Teacher' and 'Lord,' and rightly so, for that is what I am. Now that I, your Lord and Teacher, have washed your feet, you also should wash one another's feet. I have set you an example that you should do as I have done for you. Very truly I tell you, servants are not greater than their master, nor are messengers greater than the one who sent them. Now that you know these things, you will be blessed if you do them." (Jn 13:1-5, 12-17)

In the emerging culture, the most important quality of a leader is the ability to give up one's power and replace it with compassion. Jesus showed his love for the disciples by serving them. As one author says, "We can serve without loving, but we cannot love without serving."[14] Since so many of the emerging leaders are coming into leadership with pain, brokenness and loneliness in their lives, what is the role of existing leaders in helping them be healed of their woundedness?

Hospitality: A Leadership Gift

In *The Wounded Healer* Henri Nouwen asks the question "How does healing take place?" He goes on to say that although many words, such as *compassion, understanding, fellowship* and *community,* have been used to describe the "wounded healer" leader, he suggests the word *hospitality.*[15] Hospitality seems like a strange characteristic for a leader. However, if you look at what Jesus did during the Last Supper (as well as at many other times during his ministry), he was exercising the gift of hospitality. He was creating an environment where the disciples and others could be cared for in a time of need. Jesus provided the ultimate gift of hospitality through providing the means to be restored to relationship with God the Father through his death on the cross.

One of the gifts required for bishops in the early church was the gift of hospitality. Is providing hope and care for others through the gift of hospitality high on our list of qualifications for a leader? Hospitality that leads to relationships cannot be rushed. It requires time. More and more we will see that the organization of the future will be relationship centered. It will be led by people who always find time for people. Studies have shown that none of the leaders of the top-performing organizations are top-down, take-charge leaders. They place little reliance on positional authority. Their power comes from fostering relationships between themselves and others. In addition, they assist others in building relationships among themselves. James Heskitt suggests we add "relational power" to the lexicon.[16]

Relational Authority

Emerging leaders reject positional authority in favor of relational authority. The emergent movement as a whole is generally suspicious of traditional forms of leadership. For them, leadership and the accompanying power that comes along with it, should stem more from relationships and less from positional authority. They want existing leaders not to be "over" them but "among" them. This view of authority aligns with the New Testament teaching on the priesthood of believers and Jesus' teaching that the greatest among you must be the servant of all.[17] The apostle Paul described Jesus' view of relational or servant leadership in the letter he wrote to the church in Philippi.

> [Jesus], being in very nature God,
> did not consider equality with God something to be used to
>   his own advantage;
> rather, he made himself nothing
> by taking the very nature of a servant,
> being made in human likeness.
> And being found in appearance as a human being,
> he humbled himself
> by becoming obedient to death
> —even death on a cross! (Phil 2:6-8)

As Jesus modeled earned authority through a servant attitude, so emerging leaders today look to the existing leaders to have the same type of attitude. Emerging leaders recognize that Jesus did not lead through the use of titles. Jesus and the disciples did not have a senior pastor, senior discipler or a senior fisher of men. What do these titles signal to emerging leaders? They signal power, not servanthood. Emerging leaders realize that genuine authority comes not from a designated position but from a servant's attitude. Existing leaders will want to recognize that leadership change in the emerging culture. Tom would be much more willing to follow George's leadership if George were willing to come alongside Tom rather than speak down to Tom.

> **Power is taken.**
>
> **Authority is granted.**
>
> **Leadership is exercised.**
>
> KEVIN FORD,
> *Transforming Church*

Linus Torvaldo, the inventor of Linux, has this type of earned authority. Although he presides over the largest collaborative project in history, he holds no ownership rights beyond the name and no royalties. He has no positional authority over the more than ten thousand programmers who have worked on the project. He only has influence. His power is based on respect, not position.[18] Linus would probably agree with Jim Collins, who states:

> The practice of leadership is not the same as the exercise of power. If I put a loaded gun to your head, I can get you to do things you might not otherwise do, but I have not practiced leadership. I've exercised power. True leadership only exists if people follow when they have the freedom not to. If people follow you because they have no choice, then you are not leading.[19]

Shared Power Leads to Trust

For emerging leaders, leadership comes when power is shared rather than authority exerted. Building trust through relationship is the foundation for shared power. As Gary Collins, a leading

Christian psychologist, found out, relationships take time. "'I don't want to be somebody's project,' a young man said to me recently over lunch. We had taken over a year to build a friendship, a year for me to earn his trust. . . . He wants a relationship with a caring friend."[20] These emerging leaders are seeking existing leaders who are mentors and coaches, not just managers. They are looking for leaders who lead more by relational persuasion than by command. As we will see in the next chapter, they are also drawn toward organizations and leaders that create a genuine sense of community.

The emerging leaders are looking for mentors and for spiritual direction. As Dan Kimball reminds us,

> What we need to grasp is that emerging generations are hungering for a spiritual experience, for spiritual leaders to point them toward God. Think of what a clash of values it is to offer them an executive director of finances, a senior pastor, or an executive associate pastor when they are looking for a prophet, a rabbi, a spiritual mystic, a philosopher, a shaman. . . .
>
> [T]he Greek word [for pastor] *piomen* means "a shepherd, one who tends herds or flocks."
>
> Won't people in the emerging culture be drawn to this type of leader? A pastor who tenderly cares for and loves them?[21]

As existing leaders show their concern for the younger leaders, then the younger leaders will convey authority to the existing leader. Existing leaders should recognize that unless the emerging leaders choose to follow them, the team will not go anywhere. The New York Giants coach Tom Coughlin had to learn that lesson before his team could win the Super Bowl.

The leader is tied to the team. True leadership is given (earned), not taken (position). Walter Wright describes leadership as a "relationship of influence perceived by others who choose to follow. It is a delegation of trust given by the follower."[22] One of the critical tensions between George, the senior pastor, and Tom, the emerging leader, was that George had not taken the time to earn Tom's trust. George had assumed Tom's trust because George was the senior pastor. If George and Tom are going to be able to partner in ministry together, they are going to have to develop trust with each other.

Trust is the foundation of the leader's relationship with the team. Trust has to be earned. Trust is essential for the cohesion of the team. Without it, the team cannot move forward. It is the glue that holds the team together. Good leaders lead by trust rather than coercion. If trust abounds, then the team can work together. Therefore, one of the primary roles of the leader is to build trust and credibility. Kevin Ford states, "Trust is the starting point for shared ministry. . . . I have seen leaders fail because their passion for change far exceeded the trust they had earned. Building trust requires time."[23] When trust happens, the leader can move the organization in change. In a recent study it was discovered that the difference between the top 20 percent of leaders and the bottom 20 percent was their ability to develop trust. In the top 20 percent, trust allowed the leaders to communicate and implement necessary change.[24]

In the past, leaders have been taught to lead with their heads, not their hearts. Leaders were supposed to not get too close to those they led. However, as we have moved into this new culture, and ever since the catastrophic September 11 events, leaders of companies have embraced a more compassionate style of leadership, leading with the heart, not just the head. Part of leading with the heart and building trust is to be a compassionate leader. A simple definition of compassion is putting others' needs before one's own. No longer will facts and numbers be the sole basis for making decisions. As Dave Ulrich explains, the leader of the future will be known for the following:

> Less for what they say and more for what they deliver
> Less by their title and position and more by their expertise . . .
> Less by what they control and more by what they shape
> Less by goals they set and more by mind-sets they build.[25]

Changes to Consider

1. What changes should existing leaders make to change from a hierarchical, positional view of leadership to a shared, earned view of authority? What can emerging leaders do to develop trust?

2. How can you change your leadership team to be more hospitable and servant oriented?

3. How can you implement a greater sharing of power in your leadership team?

Part Three

THE LEADERS'
ROLE

From Task to Community

Question to ponder:
Why is community so essential for leadership today?

A few years ago I was asked by Ty Saltzgiver, then Young Life regional director for the Carolinas, to do a leadership seminar for his regional staff team. About halfway through my presentation, when I was describing the differences between modern and emerging leaders, I saw a number of staff looking around the room and pointing to each other. I was not sure if I had made them bored or agitated or had struck a nerve. Immediately after the presentation, about eight Young Life staff rushed up to me, thanking me for my insights. I had finally put into words the tension the older and younger staff were feeling toward each other.

The two staff teams from Charlotte and Greensboro were led by area directors in their forties, while the rest of their teams were composed of staff in their early to middle twenties. For the last several months, the older and younger staff on each team had been talking past each other. They could not understand each other, because the younger and older staff had two completely different perspectives on leadership. The older staff wanted to talk about the task ahead of them, while the younger staff wanted to build a community first—before they began to work on the task. I had put into words the tensions and confusion they were all feeling.

Task or Community: Which Comes First?

Roberta Hestenes wrote a book a number of years ago titled *Turning Committees into Communities.* Her premise was that committees become more productive and more meaningful when they take the time to develop a community. Jesus offers an example in the way he developed the disciples into a community, not just a committee. They ate together, went on road trips, shared about their family situations.

More recently Patrick Lencioni has written *Silos, Politics and Turf Wars: A Leadership Fable About Destroying the Barriers That Turn Colleagues into Competitors.* Both of these books deal with the tension we face today between task and community. This distinction between committees and communities or competitors and colleagues is one of the critical tensions between existing and emerging leaders.

The key question to discuss is, which comes first—task or community? For most existing leaders, task is the goal. Developing community along the way is a nice byproduct. But community is never the goal of the group. The two forty-year-old Young Life area directors shared that perspective. For emerging leaders, community is the key ingredient to accomplish the task. The rest of the Young Life team shared that view. For them, place came before purpose. How did we get into this state of tension?

Hard or Soft Measurement

In the modern culture, which was built around the rugged individualist and the grandiose purpose or goal, we were driven to emphasize task. We would ask the questions, where are we going and how are we going to get there? The people in the group mattered only to the degree they could help the group accomplish the task. To know whether we accomplished the goal, we relied on the "hard stuff" (what can be measured) rather than the "soft stuff" (what cannot be measured). Did our church grow from three hundred to five hundred these last three years? Did we reach the target of $1.3 million in our capital campaign? We feel like our congregations and our governing boards are all measuring us on these numeric goals. Therefore, we place more of an emphasis on what is measurable. If we come to the conclusion that what is measurable is more real, then it is "easy to relegate the soft stuff, such as the quality of interpersonal relationships and people's sense of purpose in their work, to a secondary status."[1]

InterVarsity, the organization I have worked with for more than thirty years, is in the midst of a campaign to increase the overall number of students we minister among to 42,000 from the present 32,000 students and faculty. The goal is an admirable one. We have a specific task to accomplish. However, if we emphasize the numerical goal instead of the changed values and changed practices that have to take place to create an environment for growth, we may miss some of the "soft stuff" that is necessary to be the type of community God wants us to become.

When we start talking about task and growth in the church, we invariably go back to the early church, where in one day the church grew from 120 people to 3,120 people. However, the emphasis in the early church was not on numerical goals (there were none) but on attitudes and actions. Jesus called the church of 120 in Jerusalem to have an attitude of witness (Acts 1:8). As they had an attitude of witness, they experienced the tremendous growth of three thousand people added to their numbers in one day. As they concentrated on certain actions—devotion to the apostles' teachings, shared community, wonders and signs, meeting together and praising God (Acts 2:42-47)—they continued to see new converts. "The Lord added to their number daily those who were being saved" (Acts 2:47). The early church focused, not on numbers, but on people and their attitudes and actions. Why do many of us in the church today still concentrate on numerical goals?

In the past quarter century or more, the church has to some degree been coopted by the modern mindset of an overemphasis on the measurable and tangible. The corporate model had an appeal to many church leaders. As Donald Hughes states, "It allowed for order without the special demand of spirituality."[2] However, this corporate model is losing its appeal in the business world because the business leader is learning that the hierarchical, task-oriented corporate model is not succeeding. People saw it for what it was and still is: a system designed to serve the institution, not the people in the institution or the people outside the institution. Instead of focusing on people, we focused on ideas and concepts. The result has been that "we have built congregations rather than communities, buildings rather than temples of living stones, and audiences rather than families of faith."[3]

From Goal-Driven Leadership to Relationship-Driven Leadership

This tension hit home to Dann Pantoja one day as he presented the Waves Church Planting Ministry Plan in a professional way to a group interested in being involved in a church plant. After the presentation, Dann was amazed at the silence of the people in the audience. Finally, one of the people in the audience spoke up and asked Dann how this approach would enhance their community life. Dann's response was that the question would get them off the track of their task: the Great Commission. Dann wanted to deal with it later. The person exclaimed, "Church planting is all about building a biblical community. This can only be done by being a genuine biblical community. Being determines doing. . . . We cannot have a successful church plant and accomplish our church growth goals unless we become a genuine biblical community."[4]

> It would do us well to remember that our job is to help people with their lives rather than build infrastructures that help institutions stay alive. Sometimes we focus so much on building a "healthy church" that we forget to tend to the health of people.
>
> **JOSEPH MYERS**
> *Organic Community*

We need to shift from a goal-driven leadership style to a relationship-oriented style.[5] We have to make sure we are loving people and not using them, caring for people more than our goals. All through the Scriptures and church history we see the importance of community for its own sake and as the foundation for accomplishing the task. In John 10:3-13 we see the strong bond the shepherd has with the sheep. It is the same bond Jesus wants us as leaders to have with the people we lead.

Charles Handy proclaimed a number of years ago that a public corporation should and will be regarded, not as a piece of property owned by the current holders of its shares, but as a community. People who work there are more properly thought of as citizens than as employees, and they are involved with the organizational community to pursue a common purpose.[6]

We in the church world should have seen the incompleteness of the hierarchical, task-oriented model long ago. All we have to do is look back at Jesus' leadership style to see how we have steered off course. As Jesus established the church as a faith community, he chose community to be his leadership development model. He did so because he was part of a community leadership model in the Trinity—Father, Son and Holy Sprit. Jesus spent three years building the disciples into a community. Even their mealtimes were a part of community development. As Walt Wright states in *Don't Step on the Rope,* "There is something about a shared meal, going back to the biblical concept of breaking bread together, that lowers defenses and opens communication at deep and personal levels. For some reason, eating makes talking more personal. And it feeds the relationships that build community."[7]

Even as Jesus gave the early church its task by saying, "You will be my witnesses in Jerusalem, and in all Judea and Samaria, and to the ends of the earth" (Acts 1:8), he used a plural word for "you." In other words, Jesus meant, "You will be my witnesses *in community.*" In fact, in the New Testament, the vast majority of the times "you" is mentioned, it is the plural "you" that is indicated. I think the church would have a much better understanding of Christian community if we all spoke like those in the southern United States, where the plural word "you" could be translated "y'all." The task Jesus gave the early believers was a relational task of "being" his witnesses. The emphasis was on who they were, not what they were to do. In the church, being should come before doing.

From the Great Commission to the Great Commandment

Let me give you an example of this tension between task and community that many churches are facing today. Churches are beginning to realize that what motivated people in the past to be involved in evangelism will not necessarily motivate people today. In the past, and even today, most churches use the Great Commission in Matthew 28:18-20 as a rallying cry for evangelism.

> Jesus came to them and said, "All authority in heaven and on earth has been given to me. Therefore go and make disciples of all nations, baptizing them in the name of the Father and of the Son and of the Holy Spirit, and teaching them to obey everything I have commanded you. And surely I am with you always, to the very end of the age."

In the English translation, the emphasis is on "go." Evangelism is a task. The task has a high calling of going to all nations. And the task has a cosmic calling since Jesus has authority in heaven and earth. The task is between good and evil, right and wrong. And the task of the Great Commission has served the church well. Why should it not serve the church well in the twenty-first century?

One fact most of us do not realize is that the Great Commission, as a rallying call for evangelism, did not come into prominence until the early 1800s, during the early stages of the modern era. It was not a rallying cry for evangelism since the time of Christ, as many of us assume. Even the term "The Great Commission" as a heading for this part of Scripture was not used until much later. During the colonial period of the West, in which the Western church was a partner, the call or task was to westernize the world. As part of that world task, the Western church saw that its task was to evangelize the whole world. It was during this time that Matthew 28:18-20 became titled the Great Commission and became the rallying cry for evangelism. For the most part, it served the church well for the last two hundred years.

For many reasons the rallying cry of the Great Commission has lost some of its luster in this emerging culture. Now, this should not mean that evangelism itself has lost its luster. We just need to emphasize a new rallying cry that has a more relational dimension. We do not have to go far. When Jesus was asked what was the greatest commandment, he did not quote what we know as the Great Commission. Instead he said, "Love the Lord your God with all your heart and with all your soul and with all your mind" and "Love your neighbor as yourself" (Lk 10:27). The greatest love we can offer others is Jesus as their Savior and Lord. The word "your" is in the plural, meaning people are to love as a community. Jesus went on to say that the world will know we are his disciples by the way we love each other (Jn 13:35). Jesus saw the Christian community as a powerful apologetic for evangelism. The same can be said for the emerging culture context we live in today. The most powerful apologetic for the gospel today is true Christian community.

I hope you see that evangelism is only one example of how we can be emphasizing the relational or community dimension of the gospel in this emerging culture context. Task is not negated. It just flows out of community. The same can be said for church leadership. The task of church leaders flows out of the community of church leaders. In the modern world we saw community as a byproduct or a possible bonus of the task. It was secondary, not primary. In the emerging culture context, community is essential to accomplishing the task. Jesus' leadership style reflected an emerging culture style more than a modern culture style.

Jesus, Leadership and Community

Jesus' relationship with the disciples first began with a purpose or vision. "Come, follow me, and I will send you out to fish for people" (Mt 4:19). The purpose or vision was fishing for people. The means was to follow Jesus. To follow Jesus meant to be part of Jesus' community. Jesus and the disciples formed a community for three years. They ate together, walked together, spent time in discussions together. It was the bonding into a community that allowed them to fulfill their purpose. As we read above, it was the community that became a powerful apologetic for the gospel. So instead of being a byproduct, community is essential. Walt Wright describes the relationship between purpose and community as follows: "Teams form first around purpose: shared vision, common objectives. That is the unifying reason for the existence of the team. But it is the relational connection between members that makes a group of people into an effective team."[8]

Figure 1 is my attempt to diagram the difference between a modern view of task and community and that of the emerging culture.

Modern church

Plan → Task → Community (optional)

Emerging church

Community (essential) → Vision → Task

Figure 1

Why is community essential for leadership today? First, with extended family so scattered, and with most of our relationships so superficial, people today are desperately longing for community. This longing for community is not inappropriate or a sign of weakness but is a sign of reality. We were all created to live in community with God and with other people. To ignore that reality is to overlook a significant part of who we are created to be. The strength of the disciples came about from the community they had with Jesus and each other. Jesus cared for them and cared for the mission. People today, including emerging leaders, want to belong to a community where people care about what is going on in each other's lives.

I am thankful that I know of many existing leaders who are changing their view of the relationship between task and community. Margaret Wheatley, a national authority on leadership, observes that people everywhere are longing for new ways of working together. They see the need to work together because they are increasingly overwhelmed by problems they cannot solve alone.[9] Leaders of this new type of group should be ones who "epitomize the general sense of the community—who symbolize, legitimize, and strengthen behavior in accordance with the sense of the community."[10]

Architect or Gardener?
In today's changing world, a leader may have to help others in leadership understand the importance of community. One way is to change the way we describe the chief leader. In modern culture we might use such terms as *CEO, head pastor* or *architect* and use such descriptive words as "in charge" or "in control." All of these terms and phrases connote one who is over others and who is in

command. In the emerging culture we will use different terms, such as *servant leader, guide* or *gardener* and descriptive words such as "empower" or "facilitate."

Before we proceed, I want to ask you two questions. As you read the two sets of words used to describe a leader above, how did you emotionally respond? Did you think one is stronger and one is weaker? If you gravitate toward the first list of terms, you are likely more comfortable with the modern concept of leadership. If you are pulled to the second set of terms, you probably lean toward the emerging concept of leader. To be honest, I gravitate to the modern concept of leadership. My default drive when I get stressed is command and control. Just ask my children how I act when I get tired. Or ask the InterVarsity staff in my region what I'm like during the first few days of summer camp.

However, the issue is not how I feel or what my default drive is; the issue is what is required to move forward in the future. If I lead in a culture that is crying out for community and I see the strong biblical foundation for community, I will think less about myself and more about the people I am presently leading and the needs of the future leaders. For some of us, it will be helpful to think of leadership as a crosscultural journey. We are entering a new culture that we are called to live in. So, although we might not be drawn to a new model of leadership, we have to be willing to think in different ways as we are entering a new culture.

Len Hjalmarson suggests a change in terminology. "To create an environment conducive to real community, you will have to operate more like a gardener than an architect. . . . Communities grow, rather than being built."[11] As we think about the terms *architect* and *gardener*, which better describes your leadership temperament? An architect must be precise, organized and persistent. In building a structure, the architect can rarely diverge from the initial plans that were developed, at least not without lots of consequences. In the church, an architect would tend to develop programs. The architect is always active, never passive. Usually the architect is in charge and in control. The architect is certain that if we just follow the plan, the outcome is assured. Once the building is constructed, maintenance becomes fairly routine.

On the other hand, a gardener has to always be flexible. A gardener has to take into account the surroundings. What is the composition of the soil? How much sunlight does the garden receive? The gardener has to be willing to diverge from the original plans. Some plants grow faster than others. Too much or too little rain or too high or too low temperatures will continually affect the garden. Much of the time the gardener has to wait and be patient. A lot of the growth is out of the gardener's hands. The outcome of the garden is almost always in doubt. Even when the garden blooms, there is high maintenance required to keep the garden beautiful. There are no guarantees.

Coping in an Unstable World

We live in a world with fewer and fewer guarantees. We live in a world with little stability around us and usually little stability within ourselves. We live in a world that is always in motion, from people moving to new technology to new local and global conflicts that we hear about instantly because of our new technology. Our personal world is always in motion due to family dysfunction, job uprootedness or internal conflicts.

In this type of world, those of us who are existing leaders have the tendency to lead by trying to put on masks and pretending we are fine so we can get the task accomplished. The task takes priority over everything else. We push down our feelings so we can move forward, hoping our fears, pain or lack of confidence will just go away. If we dare admit our own personal needs, we might be told to "suck it up." Instead of taking the time to grow the community, we can continue with the task. The result for us can easily be burnout, anger or addictive behavior.

For those of us who are emerging leaders in these times of uncertainty, we might become overwhelmed with all the complexity in us and around us and thus become immobilized. Instead of persevering, we might say it is too hard and quit. We feel like we will not be heard if we admit the team is not functioning adequately to meet our needs. We become resentful of the existing leaders and leave the corporation or traditional church to start or become involved in a new business or ministry.

Community: Essential, Not Optional

If existing and emerging leaders are going to remain together, they first must realize that they need each other. We will want to rediscover the importance of traditional ties from the past, such as family and community. As we have been cut off from these relationships, our heart has been telling us of our need to be part of a larger community so that together we can accomplish what is ahead of us. We should realize that we both have something to receive from the other group and have something to give. Leonard Sweet describes "the essence of leadership [as] relationship: influencing people to achieve things together that can't be achieved alone."[12] We have to believe that coming together in community to fulfill a vision or purpose is worth all the pain it will take for two groups of people who have a different view of life to remain together. We have to be able to answer the questions Margaret Wheatley proposes: "What called us together? What did we believe was possible together that was not possible alone? What did we hope to bring forth by linking with others?"[13]

Some of the main questions we in the church have to answer include these:

- Is the future of the church (local and universal) worth the time and pain it will take for existing and emerging leaders to work together?

- Are we willing to appreciate and learn from each other?

- As an emerging leader, am I willing to receive the wisdom of the existing leaders?

- As an existing leader, am I willing to share leadership with—and eventually relinquish leadership to—the emerging leaders?

Trust: The Soil for Community

Whether we are talking about the social, the corporate or the religious world, the first and most important step in developing teamwork is trust, according to Patrick Lencioni.[14] He goes on to say that trust must be built on vulnerability. Team members must learn to admit their own weaknesses, failures and need for help. How do you develop that type of trust? It comes only when people spend time together. We have already looked at some of these issues in earlier chapters. One of the first gifts I look for in any new team is the gift of hospitality. That might seem like a strange gift to emphasize in this context. However, as I said in the last chapter, hospitality is going to be an important gift in an emerging culture where people, including leaders, are hungry for a safe place to belong. Henri Nouwen describes a place of hospitality as a free and fearless place for the unexpected visitor. For Nouwen, "hospitality becomes community as it creates a unity based on the shared confession of our basic brokenness and on a shared hope."[15]

In the midst of my numerous phone calls with our Virginia Tech staff during the week after the massacre, they told me about a Virginia Tech InterVarsity alumni couple who lived about ten miles from the campus. For numerous days after the tragedy, this couple opened up their home to InterVarsity students and their friends, some of whom were not Christians. The home became a place of refuge for these students to be themselves. This couple provided meals and a place for students to show care and be cared for. Their hospitality set the stage for deepened community among the InterVarsity students and their friends.

Over a number of years, the elder board at my church had slipped back into being a task-oriented group. What we did not fully realize, or maybe were not willing to take the time to pursue, was that community relationships require time to be nurtured and tended. Relationships, like gardens, are subject to entropy. If they are not tended, they will deteriorate. It was not until some of the new elders came on board this past year and deliberately opened up their homes for elders and their spouses to gather together that community began to be reestablished. These gatherings have enabled us not only to get to know each other more personally but also to get to know our families. In these gatherings we began telling our life stories. And indeed, some of us have been together long enough that we have retold our stories several times, forming a type of culture of belonging with each other. Even the new elders now have a sense of our corporate history as a church and a leadership team. The telling of the stories and the experiencing of new stories shapes our history as a team and forms us into a community where there is now trust where there was little trust before.

Collaboration, Not Competition

Previously, in many corporations or Christian groups, the leaders viewed themselves as being in competition with each other. It became a Darwinian survival of the fittest. The question was not one of how we could cooperate with each other but how we could survive in competition against each other.

Without my knowing it, in my early days as an InterVarsity staff member at UNC Chapel Hill, I was part of a competition between two models of campus ministry: the Stanford model and the Chapel Hill model. The Stanford model emphasized staff leadership. The Chapel Hill model relied on student leadership. Our national president at the time realized that these two models constituted two very different ways of doing campus ministry. So he set these two models in opposition to each other to see which model would win. The key question for our national leaders was which model would help us complete the task on campus. Both models had advocates throughout InterVarsity. The result was that for a while we became divided as an organization. Instead of cooperation, we had competition. Instead of collaboration, we had division. Instead of trust, we developed mistrust. It took many years for us to move away from a competitive ministry model back to a cooperative ministry model.

Many of our churches have willingly or unwilling set up the same type of competitive models. The silo model of doing church ministry fosters a sense of competition. The children's ministry, youth group, young adults, married couples and senior groups in many churches are battling against each other to see who gets more money, more space and more prominence than the other ministries. Sometimes we do not even recognize that we are in competition with each other. The result is competition in task, not collaboration in community.

Younger leaders will not stand for this type of division. One young leader describes his fellow emerging leaders as desiring cohesiveness, collaboration and an easygoing, optimistic environment.[16] In a fragmented world such leaders long to be a part of a community of people who work and do ministry together. They understand and yearn for Jesus' model of ministry in and through community. They want to be part of a team that focuses on what we can do together instead of what we can do apart from each other.

As leaders, we can foster this type of community by talking about us as a team, not just about me as an individual. We should talk about working *with* people, not people working *for* us. The community is the setting in which the relationships and trust are built. We all have unique gifts and abilities that we bring to the community to accomplish the task before us. We are not called to be alike or act alike. However, we *are* called to bring our unique gifts and personalities into the community, not to see if we can

> These communities do not ask people to forfeit their freedom as a condition of belonging. . . . Belonging together is defined by a shared sense of purpose, not by shared beliefs about specific behavior. . . . Diversity and unique gifts become a contribution rather than an issue of compliance or deviance. Problems of diversity disappear as we focus on contribution to a shared purpose rather than the legislation of correct behavior.
>
> MARGARET WHEATLEY
> "Paradox and Promise"

"beat" everyone else, but to see if together we can be more and do more than any of us could accomplish alone.

As we are building a leadership community, we have to be careful to allow for a diversity of opinions and gifts within the community. While more people are seeing the necessity of community, we have to make sure we do not use community to separate and protect us from others. We have to watch out that we do not form a community of people just like us to validate our leadership and our vision. We should ensure that we do not set up an exclusive, closed view of a community of leadership. Instead we want to be open to a diverse view of leadership that takes all our unique gifts and personalities and make our community of leadership greater than the sum of its parts.

Taking Time

The emerging leaders want to be part of a community where they discuss ideas without coming to a quick solution. If the church is going to change the way it does ministry, it will take both time and creativity. Tim Keel thinks existing leaders have to be willing to move from being an organization that values control, stability and the ability to quickly resolve tension by coming to a quick solution. What he and other emerging leaders desire is a community where creative people can come together, holding seemingly opposing views, to work together and come to a new way of doing ministry. If we are not willing to have these lively discussions about vision and ministry implications, then the creative emerging leaders will leave the existing church (as some have already done) to start their own churches.[17]

To develop a community of this type of diversity will take time together. As some of the emerging leaders see the critical importance and difficult journey to become this type of a community of leaders, they would say that the community needs to be defined by relationships rather than mission. As Brad Cecil, one of the emerging leaders, states, "We measure our success by our ability to maintain relationships rather than an arbitrary mission determined by a handful of leaders and driven down through the organization."[18]

The community not only sets the tone for the working relationships of the team but also is the environment where the agenda is set. Many existing leaders are beginning to see the necessity of building community to accomplish the task. However, they still hold on to the role of setting the agenda for the community of leaders. The leader comes to the community of leaders with his or her plan and asks the others to accomplish the task. More and more young leaders want to not only work in community but also to set the agenda and lead the church as a community. In the next chapter, we will look more closely at the role of the leader to direct the team or empower the team.

Changes to Consider

1. How can you move from a committee-oriented leadership team to a community-oriented leadership team?

2. What steps can you take to move from a primarily goal-driven ministry to a relationship-based ministry?

3. How can you develop long-lasting community in your leadership team and in your ministries as a whole?

4. How can you encourage the gift of hospitality to develop richer community in your ministry?

From Directing to Empowering

Question to ponder:
Why should we move from a directing leadership style to an
empowering leadership style in this changing culture?

In the beginning of this book I introduced you to Jonathan and Ken, two pastors in the same church. Remember, Jonathan had a concern that Ken spent too much time relating to people and not having a clear plan of action. On the other hand, Ken was concerned that Jonathan was more focused on the direction of the church than he was on the people on the church staff.

Part of their dilemma was that they had different views of leadership. Jonathan's default mode of leadership was to direct, while Ken's mode was to empower. Jonathan thought the way to lead was for the head pastor to be the primary vision caster and for others on the staff and church to implement the vision. Ken's leadership style was to empower others to lead and then collectively develop a vision for the future of the ministry. While Jonathan emphasized clarity of vision, Ken emphasized the building of a community of leaders. Jonathan wanted to lead through giving direction to the church. Ken chose to lead through developing community within the church. Jonathan's leadership resulted in more clarity and control of the vision. Ken's leadership resulted in more ownership of the vision. These two radically opposing views of leadership are at the heart of the conflict facing existing and emerging leaders as they attempt to work together on a staff team.

I can see both sides of this leadership dilemma. I am a recovering control freak. When I get stressed, I tend to take over and direct a plan of action, which includes micromanaging the situation. People have to get out of my way. I want things done and will tell people what to do. I have been known to tell them multiple times what to do. Things get done, but in the end I do not feel less stressed. My staff become more stressed and certainly do not feel empowered to do their jobs. I slowly began to see that this way of leading was not helpful to a younger generation of leaders.

The Top-Down Controlling Leadership Model

In modern culture, especially the corporate culture of the twentieth century, there existed a top-down model of work. The business leaders appropriated a command-and-control method of management and leadership. The effort usually resulted in tremendous growth for the business. It developed lots of leaders who continue to run businesses with the American Management Association leadership concept. The basic management functions consist of planning, organizing and controlling.[1] The senior leaders of the company, including the board of directors, directed those under them to accomplish the desired growth. The definition of management was "getting things done through and with other people."[2] Companies became stratified into senior leaders, middle managers and workers. The result was a top-down view of leadership and a commitment to efficiency and loyalty but little room for creativity.

The formula for success became "People + Results + Organization = Satisfaction."[3] The method to achieve that success was directing through command and control.

In the last quarter of the twentieth century, many growth-oriented churches adapted this business model to grow congregations. As churches (and other ministry organizations that wanted to grow) began to look around for successful growth models in the twentieth century, they turned to the business world, where they saw a growth model that worked. They also turned to the business model because many of the elders and key lay leaders of the church came from the modern business culture. Thus the business model was incorporated by most of the fastest-growing churches without their asking any serious questions about the appropriateness of this decision. Established churches began to "worship at the feet of the sacred cow of control."[4]

The logic of many church leaders was that if it worked for the business world, it should work for the church. Many of the lay leaders and major donors in the church came out of the business world. Many of the foundations and donors that supported and still support ministry organizations are embedded in the business world. They are convinced that what has worked in the business world for the last fifty years should continue to work in the church today. There is a lot of pressure from these key donors and foundations being placed on pastors and ministry leaders to make the church grow numerically. The bottom line in the business world or ministry world is growth. In the business world the growth is measured by financial profit. In the church world success is measured by numerical membership growth.

In the last quarter of the twentieth century we saw many churches experience significant numerical growth. It is not surprising that more growth in the business world or church world usually resulted in more direction or control by its leaders. As Margaret Wheatley suggests about leaders in growing companies, "If we don't take control, there is only chaos."[5] As growth occurs, "a manager is content on running the organization as smoothly and as efficiently as it can function. . . . A manager wants to approach the inevitable chaos with the tried and true methods that have worked in the past."[6]

While I was a product of the modern view of leadership just described, I am thankful that God did not leave me there. God spared me from being a control freak in ministry when I was InterVarsity's campus minister at UNC Chapel Hill from the mid-1970s to the mid-1980s. I inherited a ministry that had grown from two to two hundred in the previous four years. My only previous ministry background had been leading a group of thirty students in InterVarsity while a student at Florida State. I felt I was always catching up at UNC Chapel Hill. Every time I thought I had a handle on the ministry, it grew again. I had to make a choice. I could try to control and direct the growth and thus feel less chaotic. Or I could let the growth continue, knowing I could not control the growth or the chaos. I chose the option of chaotic growth. I might have lost control of the growth; however, I realized quickly that God had not lost control. The group grew from two hundred students in 1975 to more than seven hundred students by 1982, and that growth happened for two reasons: I was willing to give up control of the ministry and I was willing to empower others to do the ministry.

Loosening of Control: The Iceberg Leadership Style

I began to describe this chaotic growth of ministry at UNC Chapel Hill as an iceberg. Only the top 8 percent of an iceberg is above the surface. That 8 percent represents what can be seen of a church or ministry. It is the Sunday morning church service, small groups, Sunday school and other formal meeting times. The remaining 92 percent represents the unseen times of ministry, the times of gathering over a meal, being with our friends at a soccer game, caring for our neighbor who is ill.

I began to realize that the only portion of ministry I could control was the 8 percent above the surface, the prescribed gatherings. However, the real ministry happened below the surface at the informal gatherings. My role was not to control the ministry but instead to set a tone in the formal gatherings that would multiply the informal gatherings of people during the week. I began to realize that all my attempts to bring about order only brought disorder and resentment. As I let go of my control and began to empower others, I allowed for God to begin employing the gifts of others to grow the ministry. Let me give you an example.

Danny Harrell, who is now a well-known pastor at Park Street Congregational Church in Boston, was one of my student small-group leaders. Danny led a small group of students made up mostly of fraternity and sorority members. They had a number of creative, independent students in the group. And they had a heart to reach the fraternity and sorority students on campus with the gospel. Instead of trying to control them, which I realize now would have been impossible, I empowered and encouraged them as they created a multimedia show that they titled something like "What Is This Christianity Crud Anyway?" Again, if I was trying to control these students, that title would not have been my choice. However, over an eighteen-month period, they showed that multimedia show in almost all of the fraternities and sororities on campus. Numerous Greek students became Christians. And a number of the students from that small group, not just Danny Harrell, have gone on to become leaders in the church and in the business world. Instead of controlling or directing them, I had empowered them.

Empowering Others

As we look in the Scriptures, we see that God was all about empowering all the people in the early church to be ministers of the gospel. The leaders' roles were not to direct and control but to empower and give away ministry to others. Paul described this empowering ministry leadership model as follows:

> Christ himself gave the apostles, the prophets, the evangelists, the pastors and teachers, to equip his people for works of service, so that the body of Christ may be built up until we all reach unity in the faith and in the knowledge of the Son of God and become mature, attaining to the whole measure of the fullness of Christ. . . .
>
> From him the whole body, joined and held together by every supporting ligament, grows and builds itself up in love, as each part does its work. (Eph 4:11-13, 16)

Paul certainly had the stature to try to direct the ministry of the early church. However, he recognized early on after his conversion that God had gifted the whole body to do God's ministry. Paul saw the gifts God had given Barnabas, and those gifts were quite different from Paul's gifts. Paul also saw that if the ministry was going to grow, he was going to have to be more about empowering than directing.

Some of us will want to learn from Paul. When we try to lead by controlling or directing, staff members or volunteers go to enormous efforts to avoid confrontation. They tend to be overly cautious and do only what they are asked or allowed to do. "Controlling

> I have worked for leaders who led from a façade of
> omni-competence and the best I could hope for was to
> be an implementer of their vision and their decisions.
> I have also worked for leaders who, because of their
> appropriate admission of weakness, have invited me to
> participate as a peer and really lead. I'll take the latter
> any day.
>
> NANCY ORTBERG
> "Ministry Team Diagnostics"

always gets what it deserves—the bare minimum and conformity without creativity."[7]

If I had tried to control Danny and the other students, I would have suppressed their creativity. We have to realize that people are different today than they were in the mechanistic industrial world of the nineteenth and early twentieth century and the corporate world of the second half of the twentieth century. We have to realize that what works for a mechanistic industrial or corporate world does not fully work in the human world. One of the most important lessons that we should have learned from centuries of hierarchical leadership is that control tends to immobilize people.

Desire for Control in a Changing World

I thought we had begun to learn those lessons ten years ago in the church. The emerging church leaders for the last ten years have tried to help us in the church and within ministry organizations see that we are entering a new culture that demands new ways to do ministry. Why do some of our churches or organizations seem to be retreating into the top-down, direct-and-control understanding of leadership? I must admit I see some of that reversal within the ministry organization where I am employed and within the church in which I am a lay elder.

There are probably a number of reasons for this tension. For some of us, old ways die hard. In the midst of a changing world, when uncertainty abounds, we cling or revert to what has worked in the past. We seek to regain control. We want to minimize or do away with the uncertainty by "gravitating to rigidity, to a narrowing of options that pretends to simplify complexity. We desperately want to believe that empty promise of certainty."[8]

When times get rough, not only do we have a tendency to revert back to the rigidity of control, but also we look for a take-charge leader who will inspire confidence in the midst of the uncertainty. For those of us alive in the early 1980s, we remember that immediately following the attempted assassination of President Reagan, then Secretary of State Alexander Haig rushed into the White House briefing room and exclaimed, "I am in control here." His purpose was to make the general public feel secure in a time of uncertainty. Likewise, in the church today, many of us are longing for the "strong, take-charge leaders who know exactly what's going on, have all the answers, and inspire us with their vision."[9]

Contrary to what Alexander Haig expected, his outburst did not reassure the American public. It actually backfired. Instead of the nation feeling confident that democracy was at work, we began to feel even more that we were on the edge of chaos. For most controlling leaders, the real motive for their efforts is an antidote for their

> For people who have grown up with the idea of power as strength, control and top-down direction, re-thinking the definition of power is a struggle. Yet re-thinking the definition of power and how it is applied is key to defining the essence of leadership for the emerging age.
>
> **JEROLD APPS**
> *Leadership for the Emerging Age*

fear. "The controlling leader will appear far more confident and self-assured than what is actually the case. Underneath the façade, the controlling leader is terrified."[10]

To overcome that fear, leaders try to limit chaos and uncertainty as much as possible. They tend to rely on power and control rather than relationships and collaboration. Power offers an easy substitute to the harder task of developing caring relationships. As Henri Nouwen has said, "It seems easier to be God than to love God, easier to control people, than to love people."[11] "It is lonely at the top" was a phrase used to describe leadership in the industrial and modern ages. The loneliness comes as a result of the desire to control people instead of the willingness to care for and love people.

The church has not been immune to the command-and-control paradigm of leadership. As many churches were experiencing rapid growth in the late twentieth century, it was easier to manage this growth by setting up tried-and-true methods from the corporate world. Many of the leaders of large churches have been trained to lead more like CEOs than like shepherds.[12] As we are now living in a new, emerging culture, it is hard for some of us to change.

Letting Go to Allow Others to Lead

As we now have entered into this emerging culture, we are seeing churches (like other organizations) struggling to deal with this transition. We are not seeing the numerical growth that many of us saw in the last part of the twentieth century. Therefore, many existing leaders try even harder to lead by reverting to what worked in the past, because that is what they know. However, existing lead-

> Top-down technologies of control were being supplanted by web-like technologies of opportunity, which had the effect of distributing knowledge and power more broadly in organizations and in society as a whole.
>
> As a result, the dominant model of leadership was being challenged. The command-and-control, my-way-or-the-highway heroic leader who had stood unquestioned at the top of the organizational pyramid and relied on positional power and charisma to keep his troops in line was increasingly perceived as a figure of weakness rather than a figure of strength, a testament of the old order and a hindrance to the new.
>
> SALLY HELGESEN
> "Challenge for Leaders in the Years Ahead"

ers are struggling with how to give direction in a world that does not look like the world they knew in the past. It is now almost impossible to give good direction in a changing world. There are new streets and new subdivisions that did not exist ten years ago. The old farms have been destroyed to make way for these new subdivisions. As existing leaders, we have to be careful that we do not turn out to be like the old farmer who said, "Turn at the corner where the old Johnson farm used to be."[13] As existing leaders, we find it difficult to let go of the steering wheel, especially if we think we are the only ones who know how to drive.[14]

Existing leaders have to realize that we are not the only ones who can drive; there are younger leaders who know how to drive better in this new and increasingly technological culture. As we have entered the twenty-first century, the stable and highly efficient hierarchies of the past century that served us so well are rapidly becoming outdated.

This change has caused some existing leaders to fear the future. They are asking questions about their own future. But a fear of failure has to give way to respect for failure and a readiness to learn from failure. Learning should replace control as the fundamental job of leadership.[15]

There are young, emerging leaders in our churches and ministry organizations who are not fearful of the future. They also have some ideas about where we should be heading. However, we have a tendency to discourage them rather than empower them to lead. As they make suggestions for change, they run up against a brick wall of the existing leaders who are not willing to make the necessary changes. We have yet to learn that the more we try to impose control on people and situations, the more the situations become uncontrollable.

Instead of resisting or trying to control change, should we not "invoke the resident creativity of those in our organization" or church?[16] Instead of controlling, we can cultivate and coordinate others to act and lead at all levels of an organization. If we do not empower the emerging leaders of the future, they will walk away from those institutions characterized by a culture of control. "That older style of leadership [Plan, Lead, Organize and Control] might have worked . . . in a cultural context where . . . circumstances to a large degree were predictable and change was orderly."[17]

Tim Keel reminds us that to respond to this new environment we must be creative. What worked in the past does not work today. Keel calls us to be a different type of church that "empowers and unleashes creativity."[18] Tim goes on to encourage existing leaders of the church to be willing to resist the "impulse to assert and gain control over their environment when it begins to get a little funky and disruptive."[19] Tim calls both existing and emerging leaders to stay present in the midst of all the confusion and chaos and to listen to the Holy Spirit. As the Holy Spirit guided the early church, so the Holy Spirit will guide the church through this time of leadership transition.

Leaders today must see the present as incomplete and be willing to give up the comfort of doing things like we have always done them for the promise of a future that will be better. We have to help people and ourselves move out of our comfort of the present into a time of uncertainty and chaos for the hope of a better tomorrow. A key question we should ask is, are we willing to give up the seeming certainty of the past for the chaos of the present in order to live more fully in the future? This type of call to God's people is not new. God called people in the past, including Abram, Joseph, Moses, Joshua, Esther, David, Mary, Peter and Paul, to leave the certainty of their past for the uncertainty of the future. As God guided his people in the past into a time of uncertainty in transition, so he is guiding his church today.

Earlier I shared how my grandson Asher was trying to decide whether to give up the certainty of crawling for the promise of walking. Now, a few months later, he is walking all over the place. Today he would have no desire to return to crawling. However, during the few months in between crawling and walking, he lived in a time of much uncertainty. He would try to walk but would inevitably fall numerous times. Some days, he would want to revert back to just crawling because he did not want to fail. However, slowly his fear of failure gave way to learning from his failures. Asher had to be willing to surrender the certainty of crawling for the promise of walking and running. At the time he did not fully understand all that would be opened up in his world by his willingness to take a risk. For Asher, learning to walk was ultimately an opportunity, not an obstacle. If we had tried to control Asher's desire to walk because of our fear of his falling down, we would not have been looking after his best interests. The result was certainly worth the effort.

Opportunity in the Midst of Uncertainty

As existing leaders, we'll have to look beyond the uncertainty and chaos of the present to the opportunity of the future. Instead of controlling and directing the emerging leaders in our midst, we will empower them and together prepare for the future. There is nothing more encouraging for emerging leaders than to have existing leaders embrace their ideas. We have learned that there is a clear correlation between participation and productivity. When people are encouraged and empowered in their work environments, their productivity increases by a minimum of 35 percent from traditionally managed work environments.[20]

Jesus certainly saw beyond the chaos of his day to empower the disciples for the future. When he first met two of the future disciples, they were repairing their nets with their father so they could go back the next day to fish again (Mk 1:16-20). I have often wondered if the two sons really wanted to be fishermen. It was naturally understood that they would follow in their father's footsteps. However, Jesus came to them, met them where they were and encouraged and empowered them to become fishers of people. He called them from a life of certainty into a life of uncertainty. He wanted to prepare them for a future that would be very different from their father's past life and their present life. The same Greek word *artios* means both "repair" and "prepare." Whereas the father and the sons were content to just keep going about repairing for the life they knew, Jesus wanted to prepare, equip and empower them for a future life they did not yet know.[21]

What impressed me about this story is that the father did not try to stop his sons. He could have tried to control them by reminding them of the uncertainty of the future compared to the certainty of a life of fishing. But he did not stop them. Maybe he knew that the culture was changing. Maybe he knew that the old ways of doing things would not work within this changing Jewish culture that was being dominated by Greek culture and Roman law. Whatever the reasons, he gave his sons his blessing, which empowered them for the future. It is about time that some of us existing leaders gave our blessings to the emerging leaders around us.

Becoming an Empowering Leader

How do we move from a directing view of leadership to an empowering view of leadership? We begin with an understanding that empowerment changes not only the emerging leaders but also the existing leaders. The journey ahead holds as much uncertainty for the existing leaders as it does for the future leaders. As Leighton Ford shared in an interview for the *Emerging Culture Curriculum,* the existing leaders should ask themselves if are they able and willing to "morph."[22] Existing leaders will have to be givers. They will give away power, give away control and give themselves away to others.

Although I do not in any way mean to compare existing leaders to Jesus, in some ways we have to follow Jesus' example. In his final days, Jesus stated that he must depart so that the Holy Spirit could come more fully. The incarnational Jesus understood his role on earth. He understood that the future of the church depended on the role of the Holy Spirit. He understood that his role and the role of the Holy Spirit on earth were going to change dramatically. Jesus knew he had to transfer power to the Holy Spirit for the next phase in the mission.

To lead people, walk beside them. . . .

As for the best leaders, the people do not notice their existence.

The next best, the people honor and praise.

The next people fear; and the next, the people hate. . . .

When the best leader's work is done the people say, "We did it ourselves!"

Lao-tzu
The Way of Lao Tsu

Existing leaders have the opportunity to be people who have the same understanding as Jesus that their role will, by necessity, change as we continue further into this emerging culture. They will be called on to take new, empowering roles such as visionaries, coaches, team builders, champions and facilitators.[23] In the future, successful existing leaders could be known more for the gifts they provide to others than for the gifts they possess themselves. Gifts are to be given away and not to be hoarded. Existing leaders need to recognize that leading is not about their success but about the success of the mission they could create by empowering others to lead. It is about switching from *I* to *we*. It is about empowering others to succeed.

Servant Leader

This type of leadership is a call to servant leadership. In Matthew 20:28 we read, "The Son of Man did not come to be served, but to serve, and to give his life as a ransom for many." Servant leadership is the opposite of the corporate CEO model, where everyone obeys the big boss. Servant leaders are givers, not takers. They never hold too tightly to their position of power or title. They lead by learning from those they lead. They are always available to the people they are leading. Servant leaders turn the organizational structure upside down. Instead of asking the younger, emerging leaders what the emerging leaders can do to make the existing leaders successful, the existing leaders ask the emerging leaders what they (the existing leaders) can do to make the emerging leaders successful. Jesus taught that you do not have to be a hero to be successful. In fact, he taught the opposite. The greatest among you will be your servant, he said (Mt 23:11). Jesus demonstrated this type of servant leadership when he washed the disciples' feet.

The role of a servant leader requires certain characteristics and expectations. Larry Spears identifies seven characteristics required to be a servant leader: listening, empathy, healing, awareness, persuasion, conceptualization, foresight.[24] As you can see from this list, emerging leaders desire understanding, not quick analysis and solutions. Leadership in the emerging culture will be a lot more about listening than about talking. Jesus asked a lot of questions and did a lot of listening. Emerging leaders want the existing leaders to help them find out who they are rather than tell them what to do.[25]

As you see, these characteristics fall into two categories. The first category (listening, empathy, healing, awareness) orients the servant leader to the people around him or her. It provides the basis for healthy relationships to take place among the team. The second category (persuasion, conceptualization and foresight) is outwardly focused. It provides the basis for understanding the culture around them and provides healthy direction for the organization or church. The role of the existing leader is to provide healthy relationships for the leadership team and healthy direction for the organization or church.

Shared Leadership

In addition to being a servant leader, the existing leader has to be willing to share leadership with the emerging leaders. As Margaret Wheatley exclaims, "The key trait of leadership today is having more confidence in other people than you have in yourself. Shine the light on others. Ask them to participate."[26] There is a clear coordination between participation and productivity. There is an even greater correlation between empowerment and productivity. The key to motivation is empowerment. According to Ken Blanchard, "Empowerment is the creation of an organization climate that releases the knowledge, experience and motivation that reside in people."[27]

Part of that climate change is the creation of a healthy and safe environment where the emerging leaders can develop. These emerging leaders have been told all of their life that they can be anything they imagine. However, their outlook on life has been shaken by the Columbine shootings, September 11 and the Virginia Tech massacre. As one emerging leader offered, "More than the nuclear threat of their parents' day, those attacks were immediate, potentially personal, and completely unpredictable."[28] The emerging leaders, while they want to lead, will sometimes need encouragement to step up and lead.

Empowerment involves the sharing of power as some authority and decision making is transferred to the emerging leaders. True empowerment will increase the younger leaders' sense of self-worth and personal fulfillment. It will also change the leader-follower relationship from a superior-inferior power dynamic to a more egalitarian relationship built on mutual trust and support.

Sometimes we as existing leaders do not even realize how we can create a power dynamic that we never consciously intended to create. A number of years ago, in my church, we would hold the elder meetings in the office of our teaching pastor. Without even thinking about it, the teaching pastor would sit behind the large desk in his office as the rest of us sat around the desk in a semi-circle. What he was communicating by that posture was "I am in charge here." So when I became the chair of our board of elders, the first action I took was to request that our teaching pastor come from behind his desk and join the rest of us in a circle. That little action went a long way toward the elder board creating trust within the group and developing a sense of shared leadership.

One of the reasons to move into a posture of shared leadership is to help in creating an environment where creativity and experiments can be encouraged. If we are going to move forward within this emerging culture, we will have to experiment and unleash the creativity in the emerging leaders. As I have stated earlier, all leaders should recognize that we do not have all the gifts needed to lead. As we are willing to give away leadership responsibilities to the emerging leaders on our team, they feel empowered. They will be able to use their gifts and creativity to lead us further than we could have led if we had been unwilling to share leadership and power.

Deborah Ancona wrote an article in the *Harvard Business Review* titled "In Praise of the Incomplete Leader." That title would probably not have been in vogue in the twentieth century at the zenith of the command-and-control leadership environment. In the article Ancona shares that the role of the leader is no longer one of command and control but rather one of cultivation and coordination.[29] Existing leaders can offer well-structured questions even if they do not know the full answer to the questions. Emerging leaders will need help from the existing leaders, not definitive answers. As existing leaders are willing to admit that they are incomplete and need others, and are willing to share the leadership with others on the team, then together they can get extraordinary things done.

Partnership Leader

To become true partners in leadership, both existing and emerging leaders should listen to each other. In one sense both existing and emerging leaders are incomplete without each other. The existing leaders have to accept that the "exercise of true leadership is inversely proportional to the exercise of power."[30] In this emerging culture, the more they are willing to give away power, the more they are respected as leaders. As Jim Collins reminds us, "The best and most innovative work comes only from true commitments freely made between people in a spirit of partnership, not from bosses telling people what to do. . . . *You are a leader if and only if people follow your leadership when they have the freedom not to.*"[31] That partnership can grow and develop as we are willing to solicit input from others. It grows even more when we not only solicit input from others but also begin to implement the input we receive.

Emerging leaders need to see that their input does matter. Many of them feel that they are now being asked to give input but that their input is rarely implemented. Young leaders are becoming more and more frustrated because, after being asked their opinions, there is no change of action. As one young leader cried out in frustration, "If my boss asks my opinion and it disagrees with his or hers, we're going to do it his or her way. Talk about futility! I can't understand why someone who'd already decided on a course of action would care what anyone else thought."[32]

Part of the way the partnership can grow is for both leaders to admit they need each other. The emerging leader needs the encouragement of the existing leader in hard times. In an interview Leighton Ford describes this need as the "time in between dreams."[33] Too often emerging leaders live within their dreams for how ministry could be different. It is in between dreams that they enter the tough times and become discouraged. It is in those valleys where existing leaders can be true partners in ministry with the emerging leaders, encouraging the emerging leaders to keep going in tough times.

The existing leaders need the emerging leaders to be their interpreters of this emerging culture. In this emerging culture, many existing leaders are like the blind man Jesus healed who at first could only see dimly (Mk 8:22-26). Existing leaders need the emerging leaders to help them see this emerging culture not as a threat to ministry but as an opportunity for ministry. Existing leaders have to recognize that for a period of time in this emerging culture they will have to take the posture of learners rather than that of teachers. They will need the emerging leaders to guide them.

This type of partnership in ministry takes time and honesty to develop. Jonathan and Ken, who I mentioned at the beginning of this chapter, ended up parting ways. Neither one of them was willing to take the time to develop trust with the other. Jonathan was probably threatened by Ken. Ken was unwilling to see that he could benefit from some of Jonathan's strengths and gifts. Ultimately neither one of them was fully honest with the other. Both could have benefited from a ministry partnership. Neither wanted to take the time and risk to develop the partnership.

If this type of partnership is going to work, it will take leaders who are gifted bridge builders to make it happen. We have learned that for different ethnic groups to be able to partner in ministry, bridge builders are necessary to help the two groups become willing to take the time to listen to each others' stories and begin to see the need they have for each other. In the same way those types of bridge-building leaders will be useful in helping the directive existing leader and the empowering emerging leader forge a ministry partnership.

Similarly, there will be a place for consensus builders, people who are gifted to listen to both sides and bring about consensus. Sally Helgesen suggests that Socratic dialogue will be an important part of leadership in this emerging culture: "Socratic dialogue . . . does not make direct suggestions but rather elicits suggestions from others, balancing and harmonizing them and so shaping something new."[34]

Power Through Blessing

As we move along, not only should we share leadership and become partners in leadership, but also at some point existing leaders will have to begin to let the emerging leaders do the leading. Many emerging leaders hear the rhetoric from existing leaders that the leadership baton will be passed to them. However, the action of the existing leaders says that they will pass the baton only if the emerging leaders do ministry the way the existing leaders have always done ministry. Existing leaders have to recognize that power should be shared, not hoarded. A paradox of leadership in this emerging culture is that the more power is hoarded, the less power one actually has. We actually gain power by giving it away. It is a different kind of power. Instead of it being the power of control, it is the power of relationship, the power of shared decision making, the power of blessing.[35]

As existing leaders give power and thus leadership away to the emerging leaders, they are giving their blessings to the emerging leaders. In the Old Testament, one primary meaning of blessings was a transfer of power by acts and words. By giving a blessing, the existing Old Testament leaders were saying, "We believe in you. We give over leadership to you." One of the most powerful blessings was the blessing that Moses gave Joshua before the younger man was to lead the Hebrew people into the promised land.

> Moses summoned Joshua and said to him in the presence of all Israel, "Be strong and courageous, for you must go with this people into the land that the LORD swore to their ancestors to give them, and you must divide it among them as their inheritance. The LORD himself goes before you and will be with

you; he will never leave you nor forsake you. Do not be afraid;
do not be discouraged." (Deut 31:7-8)

As existing leaders give away leadership to the emerging leaders
today, they gain the respect and admiration of these emerging leaders. So, instead of being feared, existing leaders become loved. In
the movie *Patton* it is suggested that if General Patton would ease
up a little on his troops, he would be better liked. Patton's response
is that he wants his men to fear him, not love him. George Patton
would not understand today's emerging culture. He would probably not thrive as a leader in this emerging culture. He would never
understand the concept in the emerging culture that the more a
leader lets go and gives to others, the more in charge the leader
becomes.

This giving away of power can be seen as a weakness. I am sure
Patton would agree with that statement. However, we are reminded
that in Jesus we see power coming from weakness. The gospel itself, as symbolized by the cross, is power arising from weakness (1
Cor 1:17-25). In actuality, existing leaders are not called to give up
power to others but instead to recognize and free others to use the
power and skills they already possess.

Much more can be accomplished for the sake of the mission by
giving away power to others than by trying to get people to be loyal
followers. Many more people can exercise leadership. There are
leaders throughout our church or ministry who are just waiting to
be asked to lead. Will we give them that opportunity?

The Guiding Leader

The existing leader becomes much more of a guide than a general.
The qualities necessary for existing leaders will become less about

power and more about relationships and character traits. Instead of the C words *control, command* and *celebrity,* the new C words needed to describe leaders in the emerging culture are "connect, coalesce, converge, collaborate, and commune."[36] Existing leaders will have to recognize that their best success is in investing in the success of others.

The emerging leaders will need to have patience. They must understand that they still have a lot to learn from older, wiser existing leaders. Many emerging leaders, frustrated by the slow change they perceive, are convinced that they would be better off being a church planter. However, some of these emerging leaders might recognize that they are too critical and might realize that what could be best for them is to remain in an established church and be guided by an existing leader who recognizes that the future leadership of the church lies in the emerging leaders.[37]

Within this safe environment, these emerging leaders need to be empowered and guided to take risks. In an age of uncertainty, leaders learn through a journey of trial and error. We will want to create the environment that encourages the risk taking that is

---

Transforming leaders are those who are able to divest themselves of their power and invest it in their followers in such a way that others are empowered, while the [existing] leaders themselves end with the greatest power of all, the power of seeing themselves reproduced in others.

LEIGHTON FORD
Transforming Leadership

necessary and give the emerging leaders the freedom to fail and the freedom to dream up out-of-the-box solutions.[38] Failure should not be feared but welcomed because failure in the midst of a trial-and-error period is an opportunity for learning. In a trial-and-error period, the emerging leaders will admit that they do not know all the answers and need the help and guidance of others. The emerging leaders admit that they sometimes need guidance. The existing leaders should be willing to give freedom to the emerging leaders. Guidance and freedom are key traits for the success of existing and emerging leaders thriving together in the same team with the same vision and mission.

There will be many times in the future when the emerging leaders will be the guides of the existing leaders. The emerging leaders have the desire to try new ways to do ministry. They will be the guides for the future because, unlike the existing leaders who are

---

Newer, younger leaders may not want to simply manage the programs and structures others have created. New leaders may envision ways to be faithful to the mission of Christ that are worlds apart from what has preceded them. . . . But if we follow them, they may create opportunities to reach those outside our churches for Christ. If we're wise, we'll listen and pour ourselves into what the Spirit is doing rather than pushing new leaders into what we've always done.

ALEX MCMANUS
"New Leaders, Unmarked Paths"

involved in a crosscultural journey as they move further into the emerging culture, the emerging leaders are the indigenous people, having grown up in this emerging culture.

With this type of partnership between existing and emerging leaders, the church can move forward as God desires.

Gifted Leadership

God has empowered his leaders collectively to accomplish his vision. As we see in 1 Corinthians 12 and Romans 12, God—instead of focusing all leadership on one person—is preparing each of us to have a role in ministry, using the gifts he has given us. Instead of placing leadership in the hands of one person, God has gifted different people with different leadership gifts. We give a lot of lip service to the priesthood of believers; however, our church structures often describe a different view.

If we want to move ahead to a gift-based leadership ministry, we will shift the roles of the pastors. In the modern paradigm, the leaders had the answers, vision and everything else. They did it all. However, in the new paradigm, instead of being primarily doers of ministry,

> Pastors must go beyond the rhetoric of the universal priesthood. "Every member is a minister." *You* can preach it a few times a year from the pulpit. But it is *you* who is still in the pulpit, and *you* are still seeing people from *your* office as they make appointments with *your* secretary.
>
> QUOTED IN EDDIE GIBBS AND RYAN BOLGER
> *Emerging Churches*

leaders are equippers of others in ministry (Eph 4:11-16). The former pastor of our church reminded us each year that the role of the minister was not to minister and that the role of the congregation was not to congregate. No, the role of the pastors shifts from being academic and credential based to reflecting more of a character- and gift-based view of ministry.

Trust-Based Leadership

If the existing leaders' roles are to empower the emerging leaders and eventually give over the leadership to them, then trust is essential. Like I said before, the only way trust can develop is if the leaders spend time getting to know each other and ministering together. Existing leaders need to recognize that emerging leaders will not give themselves fully to their ministry until they have personal relationships with the existing leaders.

How does this process work? Daryl Conner, in *Leading at the Edge of Chaos,* describes the process as follows: "Empowered relationships tend to foster trust between people. Trust, in turn, strengthens the relationships. Trust grows over time as each party earns the right to influence the other by genuinely considering the other's perspective."[39]

Within that relationship of trust, the existing leader gives power and leadership away. That happens by lifting others up more than oneself. Let me give an example from one of my favorite sports— women's soccer. In the World Cup held in China, one of the most spectacular goals was a fifty-yard pass from Christine Lilly, who is one of soccer's all-time greats, to Abby Wambach, the rising star in U.S. women's soccer. Abby deftly controlled the pass from Christine and hit a rocket shot into the net. At the end of the game Abby kept giving credit for the goal to Christine's tremendous pass, while Christine was praising Abby's uncanny ability to control the pass and shoot all in one motion. Christine was trying to empower the emerging leader of the team, while Abby was trying to pay honor to Christine, the existing leader of the team. It was obvious that they had built a trusting relationship with each other.

We existing leaders should encourage the emerging leaders to learn, to grow and to think for themselves. Encourage them to lead. As the emerging leaders know they have the trust of the existing leaders, they will be looking forward in ministry, not over their shoulders, always wondering what the existing leaders are thinking. Existing leaders have usually required that emerging leaders believe in them. However, in the emerging culture, true leadership requires that existing leaders believe in the emerging leaders. As existing leaders trust the emerging leaders, the emerging leaders will trust in return.

Empowering Leaders

One of the important lessons we have learned along the way is that hierarchical leadership tends to immobilize people. When structures take precedence over mission, when highly centralized leadership prevents the contribution of others, people who are gifted tend to leave. The most frequent reason emerging leaders give for leaving the church is controlling leadership.[40] The controlling individual leader of the church where everything revolves around him is a dinosaur. The problem is that the dinosaurs never knew they were a dying breed until they became extinct. This self-absorption is similar to the banyan tree in India. The banyan tree spreads its thick branches out so wide that they do not let any sunlight through to aid the seedlings at the base of the tree. The result is that, although the banyan tree itself is quite striking, nothing can live in its shadows.[41] What we need today are fewer overpowering, larger-than-life leaders, offering no chance for emerging leaders to grow in their shadows, and more empowering leaders where the ministry and ownership of the ministry are shared by all.

My daughter Tiffany, who works as a naturalist for the city of Raleigh, North Carolina, pointed me to the mission statement of the city manager of Raleigh. I think this mission statement concisely states what the leadership structure of an organization or church should look like in the emerging culture. The mission statement reads as follows:

> To build an organization in which control gives way to empowerment, direction gives way to participation and routine gives way to creativity. J. Russell Allen, Raleigh City Manager

Any organization is only as strong as its leadership. I have long said that although I have seen gifted leaders who did not have a successful ministry, I have yet to see a successful ministry that did not have capable leaders. So a logical question to ask is, how do we strengthen the leaders we already have? Nancy Ortberg declares, "A wise leader strengthens people by giving power away. . . . Leaders use their power in service of others, not in service of themselves."[42] Most of the existing leaders Bill George interviewed for his book *True North: Discover Your Authentic Leadership* had a transformative experience that enabled them to realize that leading was not about their own success but about "the success they could create by empowering others to lead."[43] The existing leader in the emerging culture will have to be more of a "cheerleader, supporter and encourager, rather than a judge, critic or evaluator."[44]

An empowering leader is one who wants to see the organization and future leaders become even more successful than himself or herself. As Jim Collins describes a Level 5 leader, he is actually describing an empowering leader. These leaders are comfortable with the idea that in the future, although the roots of the success of the company or ministry could be traced back to them, few people will know that fact. Instead they will agree with one Level 5 leader who said, "I want to look out from my porch at one of the great companies in the world someday and be able to say, 'I used to work there.'"[45]

Changes to Consider

1. What can you do differently to move from a directive leadership style to an empowering leadership style?

2. As you continue to move into this emerging culture, how can you establish an environment where you can move from the certainty of the past to the chaos of the present in order to minister faithfully in the future?

3. Who are the emerging leaders in your church?

4. What steps can you take so you can begin or continue to empower the emerging leaders in your ministry and eventually give overall leadership to them?

From Destination to Journey

Question to ponder:
In times of cultural transition,
why might a compass be more helpful than a map?

I first met Dieter Zander in the fall of 1993 at a consultation I was cohosting on how to reach Generation X. At that time Dieter was the first successful pastor of a church exclusively ministering to Gen X. A few months after the consultation, Dieter was invited to join the staff at Willow Creek Church, in South Barrington, Illinois, to explore how Willow Creek could better connect with this new generation. Dieter was hired to develop a bridge ministry from Willow Creek to Gen Xers. At first the ministry was a huge success in everyone's eyes. I remember how excited Dieter was about this new ministry called Axis as he was sharing about it over lunch with me while I was attending a Willow Creek conference. Dieter was excited about what the ministry leadership was learning as they were exploring new approaches to ministry.

Two years later, during a conference Dieter and I were both attending, I realized that his earlier excitement had turned to discouragement. Even in the midst of this conference in Atlanta, Dieter had to return to Willow Creek for a crucial meeting with

Willow Creek leadership. At the time Dieter did not share with me the content of the meeting with the Willow Creek leadership. I just knew that Dieter, who earlier was so excited about the potential of the journey that he and the other leaders of Axis were on, was now discouraged.

What I did not know at the time was that Dieter was in the midst of serious discussions among the pastors of Willow Creek about what leadership should look like at Willow Creek. The questions they were dealing with included how the leaders of Axis should relate to the rest of the church leadership. Who had ultimate authority over Axis? How did the purposes of Axis intersect with the overall purposes of Willow Creek?

Fundamentally, there was a different philosophy of ministry between the leaders of Axis and the other leaders at Willow Creek. From what I understand, Dieter thought he was being hired by Willow Creek to explore how best to minister to this new generation, with lots of freedom for where that journey might take them. From the Willow Creek leadership perspective, though, Dieter was being hired to develop a plan of how to reach out to this new people group we called Generation X, the first postmodern generation, with the purpose of eventually enfolding this new generation into Willow Creek's normal ministry in the "Big House" (the large auditorium). These two ministry views and two views of leadership caused great tension and ultimately led to a parting of the ways. Today we see that those tensions were embedded in a larger discussion concerning the transition into this emerging culture and how best to minister and lead within this new context.

The tension the two leadership teams at Willow Creek faced is similar to the tensions my wife and I face as we begin a road trip. Let me ask you a question. When you begin a road trip, are you focused on your final destination, or are you looking forward to the adventure you are about to begin? I must admit I am focused on the destination. I was so excited when MapQuest was first introduced! Here I had before me all the roads, turns and mileage I needed to get to my destination. What more could I want? On the other hand, my wife is the kind of traveler who likes to stop and smell the roses. This tension between the focus on destination and the enjoyment of the adventure has at different times caused some conflict between us.

In many of our churches we are beginning to face more and more conflict between our existing and emerging leaders over where the ministry is headed and how they are going to proceed. The conflict is similar to what Willow Creek faced a number of years ago. Are we going to focus on the destination or enjoy the journey? Are we going to lead by a master plan or a compelling vision? What will better serve us: a map or a compass?

From Master Plan to Vision

Having a master plan can bring much more assurance than not having one. With a master plan, the future seems less uncertain and safer. All you have to do is to follow the master plan, "trusting that it will bring a future unburdened by anxieties and complexities."[1] Church leaders have for too long searched for the right program or strategic plan that sets a goal or path for their church to move steadily forward toward a predetermined future.[2] Many churches and ministry organizations are still using long-range plans as their blueprint for ministry.

However, we are finally realizing that the plans that worked in the past do not necessarily work today. Those types of plans worked in a world that experienced significant continuity. However, they do not work in a world whose present and future look significantly different from its past.

Plans still have their place. They can give a direction to go in so we can learn more about the future. They just will not be helpful in getting us very far into the future. Probably nothing was as well planned as the D-day invasion of Normandy in 1944. However, General Dwight Eisenhower stated that the first thing the generals had to do once the troops hit the beach was to throw out the plan. The plan was essential to get them to Normandy. However, continuing to follow the plan would have brought about certain defeat.[3] What they faced in Normandy was like nothing they had faced before. There is a great line in *Saving Private Ryan* when the troops are bogged down on Omaha Beach. Pinned down by gunfire, one of the soldiers asks, "Where should we go?" An officer replies, "Anywhere but here!"

As we consider moving forward in ministry within this emerging culture, we are facing a situation we have never faced before. Where should we go? If we do not want to die a slow death, the answer might be "Anywhere but here!" If our ministry seems to be going along fine, why should we make drastic changes or move in new directions? A number of years ago, I was asked that same question by one of our church leaders when I suggested to our church elders and pastors that we should head in a significantly new ministry direction or be prepared to sell our building in about thirty to forty years because there would not be anyone left in our church. They would have all died! Our church, although on the surface seemingly having a significant ministry, was attracting fewer and fewer college students and young adults. We were still trying to carry out the plans that the church had developed in the early 1970s.

Instead of a new plan, our church needed a new vision. Planning implies a detailed, step-by-step, controlled process. Vision provides a more holistic picture of the future. How do plans and vision differ? Ken Blanchard provides some guidance.

Whereas a plan has a clear destination and clear steps to reach that destination, a vision has a clear purpose and an image of the future. It also has clear values but not defined steps.

As we look in Scripture, we see that God has often given his people clear vision but rarely detailed plans. To Abram (Abraham), God said, "Go from your country, your people and your father's household to the land I will show you" (Gen 12:1). To the disciples, Jesus said, "You will receive power when the Holy Spirit comes on you; and you will be my witnesses in Jerusalem, and in all Judea and Samaria, and to the ends of the earth" (Acts 1:8). In both instances God gave his people a vision but not a detailed plan. As you read through the book of Acts, you realize that no one could have planned the journey the early church took from Jerusalem in the beginning of Acts to Rome at the end of the book. Who could have predicted that three thousand people would respond to Peter's sermon at Pentecost? Who could have envisioned Saul the persecutor of early Christians becoming Paul the greatest evangelist of the early church? Who could have planned the enfolding of Gentiles into the early church and their eventually becoming the dominant people group in the church?

Time and time again on the journey the early church leaders had to change perspectives of what ministry would look like on this new adventure. Time and time again they had to depend on the Holy Spirit, not a master plan, to guide them. As Reggie McNeal suggests, God calls his people to pray and prepare, not predict and plan. That is God's role.[4]

While the vision is clear, the journey to reach the vision is more ambiguous. It involves creating an image of the future. While plans are a road map or photograph, visions are an image or a painting. While visions do not have to be complete, they do have to provide direction. This ambiguity causes us to depend on God for guidance and calls us to be creative and innovative in accomplishing the vision.

From Map to Compass

In the past, experience was a valued asset for a leader. However, when the past no longer is a good guide for the future, experience is no longer an asset. This thought goes against all that we have been taught about leadership. In the past, experience has always trumped inexperience. Experience today can actually be a handicap. Leonard Sweet observes, "Too many church leaders are relying on strategies, methods, information, and systems that are so outdated as to be barriers to leadership. The tried and true was true when it was tried. It may be false today."[5]

An outdated map does more harm than good. However, too many churches are still using old maps. When there is little willingness to relearn how to do ministry, the church "defaults to methodologies and mental maps that keep it anchored to the old world and tethered to outmoded paradigms. The anchor and rope is going to drag most churches into the abyss, cursing the waves rather than riding them."[6] Since the church is by nature a conserving institution, it is only natural that when it runs up against problems it adopts a backward direction. So instead of leading the mission, the church is tending the monument. The result is that, in trying to protect the past, we may be forfeiting the future.

A compass proves more helpful than a map when you go off road. The most honest answer a leader can give today is "I don't know."

These words allow a leader to be a learner, not teacher. This admission "forces the leader to drop pretense, drop omniscience, drop expert authority, drop a macho posture."[7]

From Tour Guide to Fellow Traveler

Instead of being similar to a tour guide (a person who knows the best way to travel and leads others to the destination), a leader in this new environment is a fellow traveler, joining others to discover the way.[8] For some leaders who are take-charge people, the willingness to admit, "I have no more understanding of where we are going than anyone else," will be hard. Some leaders would rather die than admit that their maps of success are no longer valid. That type of leadership style, belonging to the take-charge leader, is becoming obsolete. In the emerging culture, instead of more John Waynes, we need more Frodos from *The Lord of the Rings* trilogy. Instead of relying on their own strength and charisma, the Frodos of the world rely upon others.

One of the key steps a leader will want to take in this emerging culture is to say, "I am no longer the expert. I need others so that we together can move forward." In a changing world, a leader who assumes more responsibility assumes more uncertainty. Since there are no longer any reliable blueprints for the future, the cost of success for a leader is more uncertainty.[9] Therefore, a leader will join others in the journey so that they can be fellow travelers. Instead of walking in front, the leader is walking side by side with others. They all move together without knowing everything about the final destination.

While the leader may have expertise in some areas, others on the journey may have expertise in other areas. The role of the leader is get others committed to the journey, the mission. The leader's responsibility is to get people to "contribute their hearts, minds, spirit, creativity, and excellence and to give them all for the team."[10] They all should seek to "cultivate a sense of *holy* dissatisfaction— to provoke a basic discontent with *what is* and so awaken a desire to move toward *what could be*."[11] Emerging leaders often possess a spirit of adventure. They will develop a capacity of leadership that goes beyond leadership skills. Leadership capacity is the ability to lead in unknown, uncharted territories where reliable information and reliable strategies are not available.

From Answers to Questions

Leaders of the past had all the answers and knew how to tell others the answers. The leaders of the future, however, will not necessarily know enough to tell people what to do. They will, instead, be people who know how to ask questions. As Max De Pree says, "We do not grow by knowing all of the answers, but rather by living with the questions."[12]

Being a leader in the emerging culture will mean being a

> They are self-questioning types who rely on those around them for strength, clarity and purpose. Indeed, while they have a sense of the need and a willingness to sacrifice themselves, they may not even know the first step in the journey. "I will carry the Ring to Mordor, though I do not know the way." This is a far cry from the self-assured presentation of the John Maxwells of the world.
>
> LEN HJALMARSON
> "Kingdom Living in the Postmodern World"

lifelong learner. In seminary I studied under one of the most brilliant theologians in the mid-twentieth century. However, I was taking his class in 1975. I could tell that his lecture notes had not changed since 1950. This professor, though brilliant, had stopped being a lifelong learner. The effective existing leader of today cannot rely on notes from the past. The good news about emerging leaders is that they have no notes from the past. They are developing their notes as they move along on the journey. Today all leaders, existing and emerging, need to set up space and time to experience vital learning moments together by having creative conversations that create rich dialogue. The effective leadership team is one where all together, existing and emerging leaders alike, search for the better questions and provide synthesis and wisdom in the midst of the conversation.

In some ways we will have to learn like children, not like adults. As adults, we learn in set ways or patterns. We have some sense of what the outcome will be. Now, however, we will have to unlearn much of what we think we know. We will, instead, learn like a child as if we are doing it for the first time. Children have a sense of discovery or adventure because they are doing something for the first time.

Karl Weick describes the leadership challenges ahead of us.

• There will be fewer experts and more novices.

• Uncertainty will come from insufficient questions, not insufficient facts.

• Decisions will be made more by those with expertise to handle them than by people entitled by rank to make them.

• There will be fewer attempts to capture the big picture and more attempts to capture the big story, with its ongoing dynamic plot.

• There will be more focus on updating and plausibility and less on forecasting and accuracy.

• There will be more improvisation and fewer routines.

• There will be more humility and less hubris.[13]

From "Where to" to "Who With"

Part of the humility the existing leader should possess is the willingness to admit her or his need of others. When it comes to accomplishing a mission, who is on the team is probably just as important, if not more important, than where the team is going. When Jesus called the first disciples, he called them to follow him. He did not call them to a particular destination. For Jesus, who was on the team was more important than where they were going. Existing leaders have the tendency to focus on the "where," while emerging leaders are more concerned with the "who."

Too often in the past the CEOs of corporations and the head pastors of churches thought it was up to them to be the visionary, future-oriented leaders. They assumed that to accomplish their task they had to go off by themselves to a plush conference retreat to discover the blueprint for the future. They would come back only if they had the vision revealed to them and they were ready to reveal it to the others in the company or congregation. I think many existing leaders in the past viewed their role to be like that of Moses, played by Charlton Heston, in the movie *The Ten Commandments*. Their role was to go up alone to the mountaintop, obtain the vision from God and return to give the vision to the rest of the church.

Instead of that, we leaders have to develop our following skills, not our prophetic skills, in today's culture. Leadership that is not well grounded in followership—following Jesus—will be dangerous both to the church and to the world.[14] Not only do leaders need to know when to follow Jesus, but also they need to know when to follow others in their ministry or organization. The vision must be a shared vision, using all the skills and gifts God has given the team of leaders as a whole. In this case the whole is greater than the sum of its parts. The development of the vision is more like carrying out a joint art project than like building a house. Instead of a static master plan rolled out by the leader(s), an environment (community) needs to be formed where the vision can be created together.

Alan Roxburgh gives some assistance in the development of this type of environment.

• Create a common language

• Learn to dialogue outside of power and status (positions) through the development of friendships

• Be willing to step outside of cultural and structural assumptions[15]

As we have stated before, trust by all is critical in the development of the shared vision. The development and implementation of the vision will necessitate moving into uncharted territory, taking risks and living with failure along the way. Alan Roxburgh calls trust "the invisible bond or covenant, between the leader(s) and the people that makes the journey possible.[16] The trust forged among all involved will create the context for all to become part of the vision process. Working together, the community as a whole begins or continues to write its own story. It is the shared stories, experiences and memories the community develops together that will continue to bind them in covenant with each other and God and that will help them through the uncertain times ahead of them.

From CEO to Catalyst

The existing, modern leader leads through building a great empire and using it for the common good. The emerging, postmodern, catalytic leader leads through influence, using the collateral he or she has acquired through trust or respect. Bill Gates typifies the Boomer, modern leader. He has built a powerful, global empire in Microsoft that he is now using for the common good through the Gates Foundation. Bono, on the other hand, models more of an emerging-leader approach by leveraging his personal influence to encourage others toward love and good deeds.[17]

A catalytic leader influences others because this leader has developed a mutual trust with those he or she is trying to influence. The catalyst comes alongside people as a peer and meets them where they are. Such a leader makes sure others not only *feel* heard but *are* heard. The catalyst does not want to be the hero but wants the community as a whole to be the hero. The catalyst is able to not only live in ambiguity but also help others live in that ambiguity.

From Planners to Dreamers

Within that ambiguity and trusting environment, we allow for people to dream about the future. One of the great qualities of most emerging leaders is their ability and desire to dream big. "Their disenfranchisement often propels them toward a passionate desire for great change. . . . Their ability to conceive of an exciting future can be inspiring. . . . They cherish the invitation to dream."[18] Their inclination is to dream first and set targets later. When the past is not a helpful guide to the future, we will take the opportunity to dream of what the future might be.

I encourage our student leaders, as they plan for the coming year, to have a "dream session" in which they begin to envision what the future might hold for their InterVarsity community on campus. The same type of dream sessions can be helpful for a church community. Who can forget the awe-inspiring "I Have a Dream" speech by Martin Luther King Jr. in the 1960s? King did not spend lots of time planning for the future. Because there were no blueprints or recent examples of the type of community he envisioned, he had to begin with a dream. As we move forward into this emerging culture, we need to envision (dream) what the future might hold long before we can set targets or provide any type of blueprints of how we might get there.

From that dream of envisioning the future, we develop a passion to see that dream realized. Motion flows from emotion. The collective emotion builds a community-wide base of support and commitment to realizing the dream. Planning has been replaced by preparedness. One will have to be prepared for the unknown. It is easy to plan for what you know lies ahead of you. What is much more difficult is to be prepared for what you might face.

In addition to possessing leadership skills, existing and emerging leaders need leadership capacity. Leadership capacity is the ability to lead in unknown and difficult situations where reliable information is not available. As a leader, one not only has to have the ability to dream

Chart 2: Manager-Leader Chart

Manager	Leader
Conceptualizes plans by working from the present to the future	Conceptualizes outcomes from the future back to the present
Focuses on the short term	Focuses on the long term
Implements the vision	Clarifies the vision
Threatened by change	Excited by change[a]

[a]Adapted from George Barna, *The Second Coming of the Church* (Nashville: Word Publishing, 1998), p. 37.

but also the ability to lead the change process when change is unpredictable. Planning is sufficient when the change is continuous and predictable. When change is discontinuous and unpredictable, plans go out the window or at least prove only partially reliable. Discontinuous change has little relationship to the past. It occurs unexpectedly and is not part of a pattern. (The dissolution of the Soviet Empire and the 9/11 tragedy are examples of discontinuous change.)[19]

From Destination to Journey

Leonard Sweet describes the emerging culture like a waterway rather than a road map.

> A seascape, its surface is fluid, not fixed, changing with every gust of wave and wind, always unpredictable. Maps and blueprints are useless on the water, never the same. . . . The only way one gets anywhere on the water is not through marked-off routes one follows but through navigational skills and nautical trajectories.[20]

The only way to navigate uncharted territory is with a compass. Maps, by definition, are helpful only in known worlds—worlds that have been charted before. When we have only a compass or navigational tools to guide us, the emphasis should be on the journey and not the destination.

In any type of journey in uncharted territory, willingness to take risks is critical. The degree to which we are willing to take risks determines our ability to move forward into, and eventually through, the emerging culture. By avoiding risk, we really are risking the future. All the explorers of the past were huge risk takers. If not for those risk takers, the human race would never have explored many parts of the world or outer space.

As Martin Luther King had a dream speech about civil and human rights, so President John F. Kennedy had a dream speech in the 1960s about outer space. Many people thought that dream was too risky. It is the tendency of many people to be comfortable in the present, avoiding unnecessary risks. The vocabulary we use to discuss risk tells us a lot about how we view risk. We use phrases like "minimize risk," "spread the risk," "running the risk," "balancing the risk," "worth the risk."[21] Although many questioned that dream of putting a man on the moon, it was a dream that galvanized a nation. It was worth the risk.

The space race of the 1960s was a modern goal. It had a destination. Within this paradigm, the world was viewed as a machine that was predictable and acted with clockwork precision. In today's uncertain culture a better question than "Where are we headed?" might be "What are we hoping for?" "What are we hoping for?" is a journey-based question. It admits that we have little control over where we are going.[22]

From Fellow Traveler to Journey Guide

While we have seen that the existing leader first will want to move from being a modern expert to being a postmodern fellow traveler, eventually the changed existing leaders and emerging leaders together need to be the journey guide for the rest of the congregation or ministry. These leaders, as a team, will first be the advance scouts, like Joshua's men moving into Canaan to spy out the land. They will learn all they can, not only about the emerging culture but also about how to do ministry in this changing context. In addition, they will learn how to adapt the present ministry values and ministry strategies to this next context.

We will see leadership in the emerging culture as a quest, like that in *The Lord of the Rings*. We will have to be willing to take risks and be uncomfortable at times. Although this approach is filled with all types of obstacles, it is also filled with experiences of unexpected joy. The joy of discovery is the expectation of the day. Leaders become like experienced travelers. True, experienced travelers are explorers or adventurers. As they move into uncharted territory, true travelers will take risks and try new strategies in order to learn new patterns of ministry that are appropriate for the emerging context. They will leave the time-proven ministry strategies and get off the map to explore new territories. They will be willing to adapt to unforeseen circumstances and learn from these experiences.

As the leaders learn the way into the new territory, they become journey guides for the rest of the members. The journey guides keep the congregation on the path. Everyone should contribute to make this adventure successful. As journey guides, the leaders will have to convince some of the more settled congregational members that the journey is worth the effort—if not for them, then for the people who will come after them. The leader will have to have courage to move the congregation forward.

> The first and most basic task of the Christian leader in the future will be to lead his people out of the land of confusion into the land of hope.
> . . . Hope prevents us from clinging to what we have and frees us to move away from the safe place and enter unknown and fearful territory.
>
> HENRI NOUWEN
> *The Wounded Healer*

Courage is necessary to move the congregation from enjoying the status quo to taking risks and moving into a new land. The role of the leader today will be similar to Moses' role of leading his people from Egypt to the wilderness and then to the Promised Land. Such leaders will need to be like the leaders of the early church who owned the vision Jesus gave them to be his witnesses from Jerusalem to the known ends of the earth. They had to rely upon the Holy Spirit to guide them in the times of uncertainty and change. Today the existing modern leaders and the postmodern emerging leaders will have to partner together to master the unexpected and often unwanted. Not only will they be required to tolerate ambiguity and uncertainty, but also they will need to help the congregation to do the same.

The role of the journey guides will be threefold. They will

- Set Direction—the articulation of mission, vision, values and purpose

- Build Commitment—the creation of mutual trust and accountability

- Create Alignment—the establishment of common ground and areas of interrelated responsibility[23]

"Leading adaptive change is a quest. And because it is a quest, there is no guarantee of completing the journey. Real change will create both trust and resistance—often at the same time."[24] Real adaptive change will take time. It will not happen overnight. But change can happen. As it is a journey without a defined destination, it is something we do not have control over. As living things may stay dormant for a period of time before growth occurs, so the same can happen to the church as it journeys in uncharted territory.

Church leaders will have to be patient as they explore what changes they should make in their ministry to be able to minister faithfully and effectively in this new culture. It took a long time to develop an effective ministry in the modern culture. It will take some time to do the same in this emerging culture. The church leaders—existing and emerging leaders together—will have to lead the congregation on a journey to develop first a vision and then plans to minister in the future.

Changes to Consider

1. How can your ministry change from a master-plan strategy with a destination focus to a journey mentality with a vision focus?

2. How can you set up a process where both existing and emerging leaders are given the space to ask the questions necessary to learn how to minister in this changing culture?

3. What questions need to be answered for your ministry to make the changes it needs to make to minister in the coming years?

4. Which leaders in your congregation can be journey guides to help your church move forward?

Part Four

LEADERSHIP'S
FUTURE

9

From Aspiring to Inspiring

Question to ponder:
Why are there fewer people who are aspiring to be leaders today?

At a recent annual orientation of new staff—a ten-day training event for more than a hundred new InterVarsity staff—I was asked to give the final talk. The staff person who had filled this role the previous year had given a talk that the national leaders really liked because it was a call to "take the campus for Jesus." I was encouraged to give a similar talk.

However, as I prepared for the talk, I tried to imagine how these new staff were feeling after a ten-day training period, having heard inspiring talks from most of our national leaders. I began to realize that about this time many of these new staff were probably feeling inadequate about being on staff. They were probably feeling that they did not measure up to the task or to the senior staff they had been around for the last few days. And so I began to realize that the last thing they wanted was to hear a call to take the campus. What they needed to hear was a call to come to Jesus with all their fears and inadequacies and to allow Jesus as the Wounded Healer to meet them where they were and give them hope.

Therefore, I titled my talk "From Fear to Faith" and began by sharing the fears I had when I first came on staff and the fears I still have about being on staff. At the end of the talk one new staff member shared with me how, before my talk, he was ready to quit staff because he felt so inadequate. However, by my sharing my inadequacies and how often I have had to rely on Jesus, this new staff member felt he was able to be on staff. He was so thankful that I was willing to share my own struggles instead of coming across as a "perfect" leader.

Reluctant to Lead

When I was younger, many of my peers wanted to be leaders. Today, though, the landscape has changed. More and more young people do not want to lead. They feel inadequate to lead. Others feel overwhelmed by the baggage they bring from the past. Still others fear that if they assume leadership they will no longer be a part of the community, because now they will be the leader of the community.

During the last twenty years that I have been recruiting and hiring staff for InterVarsity and leading search committees in my church, I have come to some conclusions. We have to be more proactive in our recruitment of leaders, whether we are talking about recruiting pastors, Sunday school leaders or small-group leaders. So instead of assuming people will be lining up to become leaders, like many of my peers did in the past, we will have to change our perspective from waiting for people to aspire to leadership to inspiring people to leadership. We will have to invite people into positions of leadership. Invitations are critical.

Part of that invitation to leadership will mean that we have to change our expectations of the developmental needs of these leaders we invite into ministry. In the past most competent leaders wanted to be left alone to lead their ministry. They worked best with minimal supervision. That type of attitude had its strengths and weaknesses. These types of leaders were self-starters and were confident. However, this approach led to many silo ministries that had little integration with other ministries in the church.

Today fewer and fewer emerging leaders desire that type of individualistic ministry. They want to work in a team leadership model. They want to make sure their ministry is integrated with other ministries in the church.

However, many future emerging leaders have a whole set of other developmental needs. As the diagram on page 176 demonstrates, many future emerging leaders come into the church scattered in many directions. They have lots of passion for life and ministry while at the same time possessing a fear of trust due to failed relationships in their past and an inward brokenness due to a realization of their sin.

In the past we would not even consider many of these people for positions of leadership. We would not want to take the time to develop them. However, it is exactly this type of leader that this emerging culture requires. We need leaders who have a real passion for ministry and a willingness to try new strategies. We also need leaders who can understand the fear and brokenness so many others feel. Taking the time to inspire these people to lead is well worth the effort. The following chart shows the journey many emerging leaders go through to become developed leaders.

The beginning of the developmental process for emerging leaders is for existing leaders to recognize the ministry's need for new

Chart 3: Emerging Leadership Development

Beginning	On the Journey	End of the Journey
From scattered	To focus	To faithfulness
From passion	To worship	To mission
From fear	To trust	To partnership
From brokenness	To healing	To embodied hope

leadership. After that, existing leaders have to realize that the leadership potential for emerging leaders might look different in the beginning of the process. Emerging leaders might seem scattered in their focus, full of undirected passion, but at the same time have lots of fear and brokenness as they think about themselves as leaders. They will need a great deal of encouragement along the way. As they are encouraged and guided, they will develop focus and trust and experience personal healing. As they are given chances to lead, they will prove to be faithful and committed to the mission and will be willing partners in accomplishing the mission and vision.

Inspiring Team Leadership

Working in a team environment also requires a new set of leadership characteristics. Certain types of people who were not considered for leadership in the past might be just the people who would make effective leaders in the emerging culture. As stated earlier in the book, the leaders of the future will have to be less task oriented and more community oriented. They will have less personal ambition and more compassion. They will be able to lead within a chaotic present and an uncertain future.

Observing the leadership characteristics just mentioned, some leadership consultants are suggesting that many women might be better equipped to succeed as emerging leaders in this changing society. Kevin Ford and James Osterhaus have identified some of the gender differences that show that women might make better emerging leaders.

It is interesting that some of the reasons some women were not seen as the best leaders in a modern culture might be the very reasons why they could be better prepared than some men to be leaders in the emerging culture. According to Ford and Osterhuas, while men downplay doubt, women tend to downplay certainty. Women are also more willing to share their feelings and to apologize. Men typically discount their feelings and see apologizing as a weakness. Men also enjoy center stage and giving orders. On the other hand, women enjoy relationships and would rather give suggestions than orders.[1]

The Role of Hinge Leaders

Who can assist us in making this leadership jump between existing leaders and emerging leaders? What we need are hinge leaders who can move back and forth between existing and emerging leaders, understanding and appreciating the gifts of both groups. These leaders are people "sufficiently at home in the new to understand it, and sufficiently at home in the old to help us understand it."[2] Hinge leaders have attachments in both cultures. They have to be capable of holding in tension the best of both the existing (old) and emerging (new) cultures. Existing leaders who do not want to, and do not think we need to, make ministry changes will not be hinge leaders. Emerging leaders who have given up on the existing leaders and traditional churches also will not be hinge leaders. We have to discover who the hinge leaders are in our midst. If we do not have hinge leaders in our midst, we should recruit them for our church. Who are the hinge leaders in your church or your organization? We should give these hinge leaders time and attention.

We will want to listen to what they have to say, to find room for them to lead and to support them along the way.[3]

Since I entered full-time campus ministry in the mid-1970s, I have had no choice but to think about leadership development and leadership transition. In campus ministry we are continually transitioning our student leadership teams every few years as students graduate and staff move on to other ministries. As I have gotten older and my staff and student leaders remain mostly in their twenties, I have had to continually rethink how I relate to my younger staff and how I should empower them to do ministry. I have had to become a hinge leader. I also have had to be a hinge leader or bridge person in my church. I have used my multiple years as chairman of our board of elders over the last twenty years to help our church be willing to question why we do what we do, recruit emerging leaders and risk making necessary changes that at times rocked the status quo.

Openness to Change

If we are going to be a church organization where existing and emerging leaders work well together, we will, in addition to finding hinge leaders, need to have an organizational change.

As leaders, we will lead the process by both challenging the old assumptions and helping others who do not like conflict to see that the necessary changes are worth the initial turmoil they will cause. As leaders, we will have to tell people what they do not want to hear.

There will be times when, as leaders, we will have to be willing to take the criticism of those in the organization who do not want to change. Many people are content with where the church is presently. As a matter of fact, if they were honest, they would admit that they were even more comfortable with where the church was thirty years ago. We will never be able to satisfy many of these people. We are just going to have to let those people go if they are not willing to see the need for change. Indeed, if we do not meet head-on with the threat posed by these types of people, then we will not be able to retain emerging leaders who feel empowered to move the church into the emerging culture.

The Changing Role of Existing Leaders

Not only is it imperative to create an organization or church that is open to change, it is also important to have existing leaders who are willing to change. What makes the situation even more complex is that, according to a survey completed by George Barna, only 5 percent of current senior pastors see themselves as leaders.[4] In the past, and still to a large degree in the present, churches have operated more as educational institutions than as ministry organizations. The seminaries have raised up teachers but have little practice in raising up leaders. As John Burke explains, "Without leadership, the

> We began to appreciate presence as . . . being open beyond one's preconceptions and historical ways of making sense. We came to see the importance of letting go of old identities and the need to control. . . . When this happens, . . . the forces shaping a situation can move from re-creating the past to manifesting or realizing an emerging future.
>
> **PETER M. SENGE,**
> **C. OTTO SCHARMER,**
> **JOSEPH JAWORSKI AND**
> **BETTY SUE FLOWERS**
> *Presence*

church becomes a giant basin full of knowledge without a coordi-
nated Body to live out the re-presentation of Christ in the world."[5]
In times of change we need leaders to help us navigate the changes
more than we need teachers to explain the changes.

One of the changing roles existing leaders today have to see is the
necessity of having meaningful relationship with those they lead.
When you do not have those meaningful relationships, it is more
difficult to have the hard conversations you will have to have sometimes. The existing leaders must be the ones who take initiative
to build the relationships. It is the existing leaders who will have
to adapt to the ways of the emerging leaders, because the emerging leaders are likely more in touch with the needs of the growing
emerging-culture population in a church and community.

The emerging leader is looking carefully to see how authentic
the existing leaders are. They come with a widespread cynicism
because of all the times they have been burned in the past by existing leaders who tried forcing them to adapt to the modern ways
of doing ministry. The emerging leaders can easily spot inauthentic behavior in existing leaders. When they spot an inauthentic
leader, they will become self-protective and cautious in their in-
teractions with this person. These types of interaction between
existing and emerging leaders do not create an environment for
collaboration.

To create an environment of collaboration, the existing leaders will have to admit their uncertainty about the future and their
uncertainty about how they should lead. As I wrote earlier, emerging leaders appreciate older leaders who are willing to say, "I don't
know." While emerging leaders might appreciate uncertain and
reluctant leaders, God certainly affirms reluctant leaders who
are "frightened, confused and broken."[6] All you have to do is look

through the Scriptures and see all the failed leaders God chose to work through. Some of these broken leaders include:

- Adam
- Noah
- Abraham
- Isaac
- Jacob
- Moses
- David
- Elijah
- Jeremiah
- Mary
- Paul
- Peter

Reluctant leaders do not aspire to hold power. It is their desire to bless others by giving power away. They do not see their leadership as anything they deserve but as a gift from God.[7] Jim Collins calls these people Level 5 leaders. A Level 5 leader is one who is typically "self-effacing, quiet, reserved, even shy—these leaders are a paradoxical blend of personal humility and professional will."[8]

In changing times we need existing leaders to make sure they are more leaders than managers. According to John Kotter, management is about coping with complexity, while leadership is about coping with change. A manager plans, organizes and controls. A leader sets directions, aligns people and motivates.[9] Leaders should inspire others to move forward. In changing times the key to leadership is the ability to inspire others and give them a sense of something worth struggling for. They understand the changing times and are willing to think outside the box.[10] They become champions for the cause rather than managers of a hierarchy. They make sense out of life's changing times.

The Emerging Leader's Role

The emerging leader has a critical role to play in helping the church transition from an existing view of ministry to an emerging view of ministry. For the emerging leaders to succeed in this transitional context, there are a number of characteristics they will have to possess. First, they need to be passionately committed to helping the existing church transition into a new way of doing ministry. Second, in the midst of this passion they will need patience, recognizing that the present church is more like a battleship, turning slowly, than a sailboat with the ability to make fast turns. Patience will cause the emerging leaders to let go of their unrealistic expectations and ideals.

Third, the emerging leaders need to recognize that they have something to learn from the existing leaders. However, this learning can only come from existing leaders whom the emerging leaders trust. The emerging leaders will require a safe environment in

---

In your efforts to lead a community, you will often be thinking and acting ahead of them. But if you get too far ahead, raising issues before they are ready to be addressed, you create an opportunity for those you lead to sideline both you and the issue. You need to wait until the issue is ripe, or ripen it yourself. True, patience is not a virtue typically associated with people passionate about what they are doing. But holding off until the issue is ready may be critical in mobilizing people's energy and getting yourself heard.

RONALD HEIFETZ AND MARTY LINSKY
Leadership on the Line

> Modernism came at life through logic. . . . We assumed
> that to each human problem there existed a neat answer
> like a geometric proof; if we just thought harder and
> got more data, then we could find "The Answer." The
> twenty-first century has shined the spotlight in the
> limitations of modernity. Most of life is messy. . . . Rarely
> can major life issues be resolved simply by acquiring
> more knowledge. Sorting out how to live life well and
> how to lead Christ's church well demands wisdom.
> Younger people, who more fully embrace a postmodern
> mentality, by and large prefer to learn through dialogue
> and discussion rather than through lecture. Why?
> Because they're not after facts. . . . They are after wisdom.
>
> ROWLAND FORMAN, JEFF JONES AND BRUCE MILLER
> *The Leadership Baton*

which to grow. This trust takes place best in the form of a community of leaders. Within that community, the existing leaders will want to develop meaningful relationships with the younger leaders. One of the ways that meaningful relationships are developed is by having fun with each other. As those relationships develop, the emerging leaders can feel safe and be free to admit areas where they need help.

The emerging leaders will need reassurances that they are both well cared for and well respected. Many of the leaders of the future come with issues of poor self-image that can be addressed by encouraging them. Emerging leaders can be cared for by assisting them in their personal and professional development.

Emerging leaders want assurance that their opinions matter and are listened to. One way existing leaders can show them the respect they desire and deserve is by abandoning traditional practices of hierarchy, power and bureaucracy. Another way to show respect to the emerging leaders is through changing the way we communicate with each other.

Partnership Between Existing and Emerging Leaders

The beginning of partnership is the admission by both existing and emerging leaders that they need each other. We should capitalize on the entrepreneurial spirit of the younger leaders and the insight of experienced leaders. The existing leaders should take the first step in inviting emerging leaders into partnership with them. Part of the invitation is the acknowledgement that existing leaders do not have all the answers and the recognition that the emerging leaders have many of the answers and wisdom the church needs to move forward in ministry within an emerging culture context. Existing leaders need to share, not patronize emerging leaders. Allow them to lead in areas where they have more expertise. As John Burke states, we have to remind ourselves to let go of the "traditional thinking that leadership belongs to gray-haired men with positional power."[11]

We also have to let go of the concept that leadership is a solo act. The foundation of leadership is a relationship between people working together in community. Developing mutually supportive relationships between existing and emerging leaders is critical. With this type of support and community, more people will be inspired to be leaders. As one young leader responded to the question of why he was willing to be a leader: "I said yes, not because I thought of myself as a leader but because I knew other leaders around me would help me grow into what I needed to be."[12]

If we are going to move forward in ministry together, the church must have a high commitment to developing new types of leaders. If we only develop leaders like our existing leaders, then we will not be equipped to move forward and lead the church in this emerging culture. We will have to inspire the potential emerging leaders to want to lead and will have to give them space to lead.

Changes to Consider

1. What can you do differently to inspire more potential emerging leaders to be willing to be leaders?

2. Who are the potential hinge leaders in your ministry? How can you recruit more hinge leaders and position them to lead?

3. What changes can you make so existing and emerging leaders can partner together?

4. What process can you establish to develop your emerging leaders and eventually give over leadership to them?

Epilogue

Not today. Not tomorrow. Not even next week or next month. Probably not even next year or in the next five years. However, within the next ten years, we will know. Within the next ten years, we will know what direction the church will go in. We are at a crossroads. The decisions that we make within the next ten years will determine the direction for the church for the next fifty years and more.

Within the next ten years, many of the senior leaders of our churches will retire. A whole new generation of leaders will take their place. What is still to be determined is whether this new generation of church leaders will take over the vacated positions in our existing churches or start their own churches.

In many ways the church today is sitting on the western side of the Appalachian Mountains trying to decide whether it will allow its energy to jump over the mountains and empower the fledgling nor'easter trying to form off the Carolina coast. The fledgling nor'easter is waiting to see if it will receive the assistance from the once-powerful storm that is now bouncing against the Appalachian Mountains. There is no question that the fledgling nor'easter will move up the coast. There is no question that the once-powerful storm from the west will eventually die. The only real question is whether the once-powerful storm will send its energy over the mountains to become the energy source to form a powerful nor'easter or whether the nor'easter will be left on its own to proceed up the coast as a much weaker storm.

The question for church leaders today is different from the question asked ten to fifteen years ago. In the 1990s we were asking the question, are we heading into a postmodern or emerging culture? Today, except for a few holdouts, all agree that the answer is yes— we are in the midst of a transition into a new culture. And so the question we are wrestling with now is, how is the church going to respond to this transition? Does this emerging culture present a crisis to the church that we must withstand? Or does it present an opportunity for the church that we must seize? How we answer these two questions will eventually determine whether existing leaders and emerging leaders partner together in the present and future to develop a powerful church or go their separate ways, neither as powerful separately as they could be together.

Many existing leaders are concerned that the emerging leaders will not only seize the opportunity to minister within the emerging culture but also will be seized by the culture and become absorbed by the culture. On the other hand, emerging leaders are getting impatient with the existing leaders who are standing outside, afraid to enter into the emerging culture lest they get tainted.

How do we break this impasse? First, existing and emerging leaders should talk to each other instead of ignoring each other or throwing grenades at each other. The type of dialogue that is needed is not happening. Whether we are talking about existing and emerging church leaders within a given church or about national existing and emerging leaders, we have to set up a mechanism for these two groups to talk with each other.

Second, as existing and emerging leaders gather together nationally, they should be discussing the broad theological and sociological implications for the church as we move into this emerging culture. There is presently no mechanism in place for this type of dialogue to take place. The Leadership Network was initially a place where this dialogue took place. However, there was a parting of the ways between the existing leaders network and the emerging leaders network. The National Pastors Convention for a couple of years hosted a joint conference for existing and emerging leaders. However, even though they were at the same location, there was little real dialogue between the two groups. Dialoguing on the larger issues is critical. The national dialogue is critical to decide if we are going to move ahead together or separately.

In addition to a new leadership structure, existing and emerging leaders should journey together to discover what ministry changes need to occur to effectively and faithfully minister within the emerging culture. The strategies of the past will have to be pushed aside. Existing and emerging leaders together will have to relearn how to communicate, disciple and evangelize within this changing culture. Existing leaders will have to allow the emerging leaders to lead us as we explore new ways to minister.

Not only will existing leaders need emerging leaders to take the lead in the exploration of new ministry strategies, but existing leaders will also need to empower the emerging leaders to eventually become the primary leaders of the church. We have to inspire these potential emerging leaders to be willing to lead. Then the existing leaders will have to be willing to step aside and bless these emerging leaders as they lead the church of the future.

Let us pray for God's guidance as he takes his church and his church leaders into the future.

Notes

Chapter 1: The Leadership Dilemma

[1]Ron Carucci, *Leadership Divided* (San Francisco: Jossey-Bass, 2006), p. 157.

[2]Margaret Wheatley, *Finding Our Way: Leadership for an Uncertain Time* (San Francisco: Berrett-Koehler, 2005), p. 164.

[3]Tim Keel, *Intuitive Leadership: Embracing a Paradigm of Narrative Metaphor and Chaos* (Grand Rapids: Baker, 2007), p. 200.

[4]Ibid.

[5]James Hunter, *The World's Most Powerful Leadership Principle* (Colorado Springs: WaterBrook, 2004), p. 15.

[6]Ibid., p. 167.

[7]Jimmy Long, *Emerging Hope* (Downers Grove, Ill.: InterVarsity Press, 2004), pp. 53-59.

Chapter 2: The Church's Dilemma

[1]Thomas Friedman, *The Olive Tree and the Lexus* (New York: Farrar, Strauss & Giroux, 2000), p. xiii.

[2]Carl Raschke, *The Next Reformation* (Grand Rapids: Baker, 2004), p. 157.

[3]Bill Gates, quoted in Warren Bennis, "The Future Has No Shelf Life," in *On Mission and Leadership*, ed. Frances Hesselbein and Rob Johnston (San Francisco: Jossey-Bass, 2002), p. 3.

[4] Eddie Gibbs and Ryan Bolger, *Emerging Churches* (Grand Rapids: Baker Academic, 2005), p. 215.

[5]I suggest you begin by reading the first three chapters in Jimmy Long, *Emerging Hope: A Strategy for Reaching Postmodern Generations* (Downers Grove, Ill.: InterVarsity Press, 2004).

[6]Leonard Sweet, "New Maps for an Ancient Future," *Explorer,* June 10, 2000, p. 8.

[7]Alan Roxburgh, *The Sky Is Falling* (Eagle, Idaho: ACI Publishing, 2006), p. 35.

[8]William Easum, *Sacred Cows Make Gourmet Burgers* (Nashville: Abingdon, 1995), p. 36.

[9]Jimmy Long, *The Emerging Culture Curriculum Kit* (Downers Grove, Ill.: InterVarsity Press, 2005), introductory module.

[10]Peter Drucker, *Landmarks of Tomorrow* (New Brunswick, N.J.: Transaction Publishers, 1996), p. 268.

[11]Erwin McManus, *The Unstoppable Force* (Loveland, Colo.: Group, 2001), pp. 74-75.

[12]Margaret Wheatley, *Finding Our Way: Leadership for an Uncertain Time* (San Francisco: Berrett-Koehler, 2005), p. 178, italics in original.

[13]Eddie Gibbs, *LeadershipNext* (Downers Grove, Ill.: InterVarsity Press, 2005), pp. 9-10.

[14]Charles Handy, *The Age of Paradox* (Boston: Harvard Business School Press, 1994), p. 37.

[15]George Hunsberger, "Leaders in the Missional Church," *The Gospel and Our Culture* 10, no. 2 (June 1998): 6-7.

[16]Ronald Heifetz and Marty Linsky, *Leadership on the Line* (Boston: Harvard Business School Press, 2006), p. 2.

[17]Roxburgh, *Sky Is Falling,* p. 21.

[18]Ibid., p. 40.

[19]Peter Senge, C. Otto Scharmer, Joseph Jaworski and Betty Sue Flowers, *Presence* (New York: Doubleday, 2004), p. 86.

[20]Irene Sanders, *Strategic Thinking and the New Science* (New York: Free Press, 1998), p. 121.

[21]Albert Einstein, quoted in Wheatley, *Finding Our Way,* p. 3.

[22]James Osterhaus, Joseph Jurkowski and Todd Hahn, *Thriving Through Ministry Conflict* (Grand Rapids: Zondervan, 2005), p. 133.

[23]Kevin Ford, *Transforming Church* (Carol Stream, Ill.: Tyndale House, 2007), p. 101.

[24]Jimmy Long, *Emerging Hope: A Strategy for Reaching Postmodern Generations* (Downers Grove, Ill.: InterVarsity Press, 2004), p. 63.

[25]Dee Hock, "The Art of Chaordic Leadership," *Leader to Leader* (winter 2000): 21.

[26]Alan Roxburgh and Fred Romanuk, *The Missional Leader* (San Francisco: Jossey-Bass, 2006), p. 7.

[27]Ibid.

[28]Sanders, *Strategic Thinking,* p. 109.

[29]Ibid., p. 110.

Chapter 3: From Heroic to Post-Heroic Leadership

[1]Dan Allender, *Leading with a Limp* (Colorado Springs: WaterBrook, 2006), pp. 60-61.

[2]Joyce Fletcher, "The Greatly Exaggerated Demise of Heroic Leadership," *Center for Gender in Organizations Insights,* August 2002, p. 1.

[3]Andy Stanley, quoted in Marshall Shelley, "State of the Art: An Interview with Andy Stanley," *Leadership* (spring 2006): 27.

[4]David Bradford and Allan Cohen, *Power Up: Transforming Organizations Through Shared Leadership* (New York: Wiley & Sons, 1998), p. 49.

[5]Ronald Heifetz and Marty Linsky, *Leadership on the Line* (Boston: Harvard Business School Press, 2006), p. 100.

[6]Jim Collins, "What Comes Next?" *Inc.* (October 1997), p. 48.

[7]Heifetz and Linsky, *Leadership on the Line,* p. 4.

[8]Bradford, *Power Up,* p. 49.

[9]Ibid., p. 55.

[10]Peter Dickens, "Incarnational Leadership in a Postmodern Culture" (unpublished paper).

[11]Ken Blanchard, "Effective Churches and Team Leadership," *Next* 5, no. 3 (1999): 1.

[12]Walter Wright, *Don't Step on the Rope* (Bletchley, U.K.: Paternoster, 2005), p. 14.

[13]Eddie Gibbs, *LeadershipNext* (Downers Grove, Ill.: InterVarsity Press, 2005), p. 126.

[14]Jim Collins, *Good to Great* (New York: HarperCollins, 2001), p. 21.

[15]Ibid., p. 42.

[16]Ibid.

[17]Cathy Greenburg-Walt and Alastair G. Robertson, "The Evolving Role of Executive Leadership," in *The Future of Leadership,* ed. Warren Bennis, Gretchen M. Spreitzer and Thomas G. Cummings (San Francisco: Jossey-Bass, 2001), p. 140.

[18]Collins, "What Comes Next," p. 48.

[19]Wright, *Don't Step on the Rope,* p. 6.

[20]Allender, *Leading with a Limp,* p. 61.

[21]John Huey, "The New Post-Heroic Leadership," *Fortune,* February 21, 1994, p. 44.

Chapter 4: From Guarded to Vulnerable

[1]Spencer Burke with Colleen Pepper, *Making Sense of Church* (Grand Rapids: Zondervan, 2006), p. 36.

[2]Edgar Schein, *Organizational Culture and Leadership* (San Francisco: Jossey-Bass, 1992), p. 33.

[3]Pat Springle, "Creating a Culture of Balance," A Leadership Network Paper, p. 15 <www.leadnet.org/downloads/file_400.pdf>.

[4]Pat Springle, "Communicating with the Postmodern Culture," A Leadership Network Paper, p. 2 <www.leadnet.org/downloads/Communicating%20With%20the%20Postmodern%20Culture.pdf>.

[5]Patrick Lencioni, "The Trouble with Teamwork," *Leader to Leader* (summer 2003): 37.

[6]Ron A. Carucci, *Leadership Divided* (San Francisco: Jossey-Bass, 2006) p. 37, italics in original.

[7]Kerry Bunker, "Leading in Times of Transition," *Leading Effectively*, October 2005, p. 1.

[8]Scott Rodin, "Becoming a Leader of No Reputation" (unpublished paper).

[9]Mike Foss, "Authentic Leadership and the Call of God," *Next* 5, no. 4 (1999): 2.

[10]Rob Goffee and Gareth Jones, *Why Should Anyone Be Led by You?* (Boston: Harvard Business School Press, 2003), pp. 18-20.

[11]Springle, "Communicating with the Postmodern Culture," p. 2.

[12]Irene Sanders, *Strategic Thinking and the New Science* (New York: Free Press, 1998), p. 155.

[13]Brian McLaren, "Dorothy on Leadership," *Rev!* November-December 2000, p. 2.

[14]John Burke, *No Perfect People Allowed* (Grand Rapids: Zondervan, 2005), p. 78.

[15]Randall White, *The Future of Leadership* (Lanham, Md.: Pitman, 1996), p. 90.

[16]Gordon MacDonald, "Who Stole My Church?" *Leadership* (winter 2008): 91.

[17]Robert Lewis and Wayne Cordeiro, *Culture Shift* (San Francisco: Jossey-Bass, 2005), p. 19.

[18]Dan Allender, *Leading with a Limp* (Colorado Springs: WaterBrook, 2006), p. 55.

Chapter 5: From Positional Authority to Earned Authority

[1]Jay Conger, "How Generational Shifts Will Transform Organizational Life," in *The Organization of the Future*, ed. Frances Hesselbein (San Francisco: Jossey-Bass, 1997), p. 18.

[2]Ibid., p. 20.

[3]John Stott, *Basic Christian Leadership* (Downers Grove, Ill.: InterVarsity Press, 2002), p. 37.

[4]Ibid.

[5]Conger, "How Generational Shifts," p. 24.

[6]Christine Zust, "How Leaders Can Command, Not Demand, Respect," Emergingleader.com <http://www.emergingleader.com/article24.shtml>, italics in original.

[7]Richard Tiplady, *Postmission: World Mission by a Postmodern Generation* (London: Paternoster, 2002), p. 251.

[8]Mark Maske, "Toned Down Coughlin Helped Giants Turn It Up," *Washington Post,* January 20, 2008, p. D1.

[9]Ibid.

[10]Max De Pree, *Leadership Is an Art* (New York: Doubleday, 2004), p. 11.

[11]R. Scott Rodin, "Notes from the Field: Becoming a Leader of No Reputation," *Journal of Religious Leadership* 1, no. 2 (fall 2002): 105-19. Available online at <http://www.christianleaders.org/JRL/Fall2002/Rodin.htm>.

[12]Max DePree, *Leadership Jazz* (New York: Dell, 1993), pp. 134-35.

[13]Gerard Kelly, *RetroFuture: Rediscovering Our Roots, Recharting Our Routes* (Downers Grove, Ill.: Inter-Varsity Press, 1999), p. 217.

[14]Roger Hillard, "Nothing Leadership," *Allelon Institute Newsletter,* January 2006, p. 2.

[15]Henri Nouwen, *The Wounded Healer* (New York: Doubleday, 1979), pp. 88-89.

[16]James Heskitt, "Leaders Who Shape and Keep Performance-Oriented Culture," in *The Leader of the Future: New Visions, Strategies and Practices for the Next Era*, ed. Frances Hesselbein, Marshall Goldsmith and Richard Beckhard (San Francisco: Jossey-Bass, 1996), p. 117.

[17]Len Hjalmarson, "Kingdom Leadership in the Postmodern Era," NextReformation <http://

nextreformation.com/wp-admin/resources/Leadership.pdf>, p. 3.

[18]Annette Licitra, "Linux's Quit Leader Courts Success," in *Executive Leadership* (2008): 2.

[19]Jim Collins, *Good to Great and the Social Sectors* (Boulder, Colo.: Jim Collins, 2005), p. 12-13.

[20]Gary Collins, "An Integration View," in *Psychology and Christianity,* ed. Eric L. Johnson and Stanton L. Jones (Downers Grove, Ill.: InterVarsity Press, 2000), p. 122.

[21]Dan Kimball, *The Emerging Church* (Grand Rapids: Zondervan, 2003), p. 214.

[22]Walter Wright, *Don't Step on the Rope* (Bletchley, U.K.: Paternoster, 2005), p. 155.

[23]Kevin Ford, *Transforming Church* (Carol Stream, Ill.: Tyndale, 2007), p. 107.

[24]PriceWaterhouseCoopers, *Innovation Survey* (London: PriceWaterhouseCoopers, 1999), p. 3. Cited in James Kouzes and Barry Posner, "Bringing Leadership Lessons from the Past into the Future," in *The Future of Leadership,* ed. Warren Bennis, Gretchen M. Spreitzer and Thomas G. Cummings (San Francisco: Jossey-Bass, 2001), p. 85.

[25]Dave Ulrich, "Credibility x Capability," in *The Leader of the Future,* ed. Frances Hesselbein, Marshall Goldsmith and Richard Beckhard (San Francisco: Jossey-Bass, 1997), p. 219.

Chapter 6: From Task to Community

[1]Peter Senge, C. Otto Scharmer, Joseph Jaworski and Betty Sue Flowers, *Presence* (New York: Doubleday, 2004), p. 172.

[2]Donald Hughes, "The Leadership Model of Jesus," JesusJournal.com <http://www.jesusjournal.com/content/view/90/85/>.

[3]Len Hjalmarson, "Kingdom Leadership in the Postmodern Era," NextReformation <http://nextreformation.com/wp-admin/resources/Leadership.pdf>, p. 8.

[4]Dann Pantoja, "Teaching Gen-Why?" *Leadership* (summer 2003): 42.

[5]Dan Kimball, *The Emerging Church* (Grand Rapids: Zondervan, 2003), p. 216.

[6]Duane Ireland and Michael Hitt, "Achieving and Maintaining Strategic Competitiveness in the 21st Century: The Role of Strategy Leadership," *Academy of Management Executive* (1999): 45.

[7]Walter Wright, *Don't Step on the Rope* (Bletchley, U.K.: Paternoster, 2005), p. 137.

[8]Ibid., p. 77.

[9]Margaret Wheatley, *Finding Our Way: Leadership for an Uncertain Time* (San Francisco: Berrett-Koehler, 2005), p. 56.

[10]Dee Hock, "The Art of Chaordic Leadership," in *On Mission and Leadership,* ed. Frances Hesselbein and Rob Johnston (San Francisco: Jossey-Bass, 2002), p. 66.

[11]Clay Shirky, quoted in Hjalmarson, "Kingdom Leadership," p. 8.

[12]Leonard Sweet, *Summoned to Lead* (Grand Rapids: Zondervan, 2004), p. 89.

[13]Wheatley, *Finding Our Way,* p. 50.

[14]Patrick Lencioni, "The Trouble with Teamwork," *Leader to Leader* (summer 2003): 2.

[15]Henri Nouwen, *The Wounded Healer* (New York: Doubleday, 1979), p. 89.

[16]Nara Schoenberg, "Teens Embrace Hugging Trend," *Raleigh News and Observer,* October 10, 2007, p. E14.

[17]Tim Keel, *Intuitive Leadership* (Grand Rapids: Baker, 2007), p. 200.

[18]Brad Cecil, quoted in Eddie Gibbs and Ryan Bolger, *Emerging Churches* (Grand Rapids: Baker Academic, 2005), p. 195.

Chapter 7: From Directing to Empowering

[1]*Essentials of Management: Participant Workbook* (New York: American Management Association, 1977), p. 10.

[2]Ibid., p. 5.

[3]Ibid., p. 7.

[4]William Easum, *Sacred Cows Make Gourmet Burgers* (Nashville: Abingdon, 1995), p. 9.

[5]Margaret Wheatley, *Finding Our Way: Leadership for an Uncertain Time* (San Francisco: Berrett-Koehler, 2005), p. 126.

[6]Dan Allender, *Leading with a Limp* (Colorado Springs: WaterBrook, 2006), p. 58.

[7]Ibid., p. 68.

[8]Ibid., p. 85.

[9]Wheatley, *Finding Our Way,* p. 100.

[10]Allender, *Leading with a Limp,* p. 69.

[11]Henri Nouwen, *In the Name of Jesus* (New York: Crossroad, 1989), p. 77.

[12]Sally Morgenthaler, "Leadership in a Flattened World," in *An Emergent Manifesto of Hope,* ed. Doug Pagitt and Tony Jones (Grand Rapids: Baker, 2007), p. 180.

[13]Leonard Sweet, *Summoned to Lead* (Grand Rapids: Zondervan, 2004), p. 161.

[14]Charles Handy, *The Age of Unreason* (Boston: Harvard Business School Press, 1989), p. 131.

[15]Ibid., p. 127.

[16]Wheatley, *Finding Our Way,* p. 28.

[17]Eddie Gibbs, *LeadershipNext* (Downers Grove, Ill.: InterVarsity Press, 2005), p. 13.

[18]Tim Keel, *Intuitive Leadership* (Grand Rapids: Baker, 2007), pp. 199-200.

[19]Ibid., p. 240.

[20]Margaret Wheatley, "Goodbye, Command and Control," *Leader to Leader* (summer 1997): 1.

[21]Leonard Sweet, *Aqua Church* (Loveland, Colo.: Group, 1999), p. 187.

[22]Leighton Ford, "Leadership Interview," in *The Emerging Culture Curriculum Kit,* ed. Jimmy Long (Downers Grove, Ill.: InterVarsity Press, 2004).

[23]Lynn Offermann, "Empowerment," in *Encyclopedia of Leadership,* ed. George R. Goethals, Georgia J. Sorenson and James MacGregor Burns (Thousand Oaks, Calif.: Sage, 2004), p. 435.

[24]Larry Spears, "Practicing Servant-Leadership," *Leader to Leader* (fall 2004): 3.

[25]Dan Kimball, *The Emerging Church* (Grand Rapids: Zondervan, 2002), p. 235.

[26]Margaret Wheatley, quoted in Leonard Sweet, "New Maps for an Ancient Future," *Explorer,* June 10, 2000, p. 9.

[27]Ken Blanchard, *Leading at a Higher Level* (Saddle River, N.J.: Prentice-Hall, 2006), p. 67.

[28]Nadira Hira, "Attracting the Twentysomething Worker," *Fortune,* May 15, 2007, p. 45.

[29]Deborah Ancona, "In Praise of the Incomplete Leader," *Harvard Business Review,* February 2007, p. 99.

[30]Jim Collins, "And the Walls Came Tumbling Down," in *Leading Beyond the Walls,* ed. Frances Hesselbein (San Francisco: Jossey-Bass, 1999), p. 25.

[31]Ibid., italics in original.

[32]Marilyn Kennedy, "Managing the Deliberately Mute," *Physician Executive* (January–February 2000): 69.

[33]Leighton Ford, "Leadership Interview."

[34]Sally Helgesen, "Dissolving Boundaries in the Era of Knowledge and Custom Work," in *Leading Beyond the Walls,* ed. Frances Hesselbein (San Francisco: Jossey-Bass, 1999), pp. 54-55.

[35]Jerold Apps, *Leadership for the Emerging Age* (San Francisco: Jossey-Bass, 1994), p. 144.

[36]Rex Miller, *The Millennium Matrix* (San Francisco: Jossey-Bass, 2002), p. 148.

[37]Angie Ward, "Better Starts for Emerging Leaders," Christianity Today.com <http://www.christianitytoday.com/leaders/newsletter/2004/cln40720.html>, July 20, 2004.

[38]Jim Osterhaus, "The New Bottom Line: Building a Relationally Healthy Organization," *Tagline* 1, no. 1 (2002): 3.

[39]Daryl Conner, *Leading at the Edge of Chaos* (New York: Wiley & Sons, 1998), p. 234.

[40]Gerard Kelly, *Get a Grip on the Future Without Losing Your Hold on the Past* (London: Monarch, 1999), p. 242.

[41]Leighton Ford, "Challenges in Nurturing and Forming Leaders for 2010," Evangelical Foreign Missions Association conference address, September 21, 1999.

[42]Nancy Ortberg, "Reflections on Enabling Others to Act," in *Christian Reflections on Leadership Challenges,* ed. James Kouzes and Barry Posner (San Francisco: Jossey-Bass, 2004), p. 90.

[43]Bill George, *True North: Discover Your Authentic Leadership* (San Francisco: Wiley & Sons, 2007), p. 143.

[44]Ken Blanchard, "Turning the Organizational Pyramid Upside Down," in *The Leader of the Future,* ed. Frances Hesselbein (San Francisco: Jossey-Bass, 1996), p. 86.

[45]Jim Collins, *Good to Great* (New York: HarperCollins, 2001), p. 26.

Chapter 8: From Destination to Journey

[1]Joseph Myers, *Organic Community* (Grand Rapids: Baker, 2007), p. 27.

[2]Alan Roxburgh, *The Missional Leader* (San Francisco: Jossey-Bass, 2006), p. 145.

[3]Ronald Heifetz and Marty Linsky, *Leadership on the Line* (Boston: Harvard Business School Press, 2005), p. 73.

[4]Reggie McNeal, *The Present Future* (San Francisco: Jossey-Bass, 2003), p. 95.

[5]Leonard Sweet, *Summoned to Lead* (Grand Rapids: Zondervan, 2004), p. 162.

[6]McNeal, *Present Future,* p. 116.

[7]Karl E. Weick, "Leadership as the Legitimation of Doubt," in *The Future of Leadership,* ed. Warren Bennis, Gretchen M. Spreitzer and Thomas G. Cummings (San Francisco: Jossey-Bass, 2001), p. 99.

[8]Angie Ward, "Looking for Leaders," *Leadership* (spring 2006): 20.

[9]Andy Stanley, *The Next Generation Leader* (Sisters, Ore.: Multnomah, 2003), p. 81.

[10]James Hunter, *The World's Most Powerful Leadership Principle* (Colorado Springs: WaterBrook, 2004), p. 33.

[11]Michael Frost and Alan Hirsch, *The Shaping of Things to Come* (Peabody, Mass.: Hendrickson, 2003), p. 92, italics in original.

[12]Max De Pree, *Leadership Is an Art* (East Lansing: Michigan Sate University Press, 1987), p. 58.

[13]Weick, "Leadership as the Legitimation of Doubt," p. 93.

[14]Robert Banks and Bernice Ledbetter, *Reviewing Leadership* (Grand Rapids: Baker, 2004), p. 112.

[15]Alan Roxburgh, *The Sky Is Falling* (Eagle, Idaho: ACI Publishing, 2006), p. 136.

[16]Ibid., p. 139.

[17]Ward, "Looking for Leaders," p. 22.

[18]Ron Carucci, *Leadership Divided* (San Francisco: Jossey-Bass, 2007), p. 121.

[19]Charles Handy, *The Age of Unreason* (Boston: Harvard Business School Press, 1989), p. 3.

[20]Leonard Sweet, *SoulTsunami* (Grand Rapids: Zondervan, 1999), p. 73.

[21]Max De Pree, *Leading Without Power* (San Francisco: Jossey-Bass, 1997), p. 138.

[22]Joseph Myers, *Organic Community* (Grand Rapids: Baker, 2007), p. 32.

[23]John Alexander, "The Challenge of Complexity," in *The Leader of the Future,* ed. Frances Hesselbein (San Francisco: Jossey-Bass, 1996), pp. 91-92.

[24]Kevin Ford, *Transforming Church* (Carol Stream, Ill.: Tyndale House, 2007), p. 108.

Chapter 9: From Aspiring to Inspiring

[1]Kevin Ford and James Osterhaus, *The Thing in the Bushes* (Colorado Springs: Piñon, 2001), p. 146.

[2]Gerard Kelly, *Get a Grip on the Future Without Losing Your Hold on the Past* (London: Monarch, 1999), p. 236.

[3]Ibid.

[4]George Barna, *The Second Coming of the Church* (Nashville: Word, 1998), p. 36.

[5]John Burke, *No Perfect People Allowed* (Grand Rapids: Zondervan, 2005), p. 306.

[6]Dan Allender, *Leading with a Limp* (Colorado Springs: WaterBrook, 2006), p. 53.

[7]Ibid., p. 19.

[8]Jim Collins, *Good to Great* (New York: HarperCollins, 2001), p. 13.

[9]John Kotter, "What Leaders Really Do," in *Harvard Business Review on Leadership* (Cambridge, Mass.: Harvard Business School Press, 1998), pp. 39-42.

[10]Danah, Zohar, "Spirutally Intelligent Leadership," *Leader to Leader* (fall 2005): 2.

[11]Burke, *No Perfect People,* p. 213.

[12]Carole Cartmill, "Don't Call Me a Leader," *Leadership* (summer 2003): 50.

Bibliography

Alexander, John. "The Challenge of Complexity." In *The Leader of the Future 2.* Edited by Frances Hesselbein and Marshall Goldsmith. San Francisco: Jossey-Bass, 2006.

Allen, Kathleen. "Authenticity." In *Encyclopedia of Leadership.* Edited by George R. Goethals, Georgia J. Sorenson and James MacGregor Burns. Thousand Oaks, Calif.: Sage, 2004.

*Allender, Dan. *Leading with a Limp.* Colorado Springs: WaterBrook, 2006.

Ancona, Deborah, et al. "In Praise of the Incomplete Leader." *Harvard Business Review* (February 2007): 92-100.

Apps, Jerold W. *Leadership for the Emerging Age.* San Francisco: Jossey-Bass, 1994.

Armour, Stephanie, "Who Wants to Be a Middle Manager?" *USA Today,* August 12, 2007, p. B1.

Ayman, Roya, and Erica Hartman. "Situational and Contingency Approaches to Leadership." In *Encyclopedia of Leadership.* Edited by George R. Goethals, Georgia J. Sorenson and James MacGregor Burns. Thousand Oaks, Calif.: Sage, 2004.

Badaracco, Joseph. "We Don't Need Another Hero." *Harvard Business Review* (September 2001): 121-26.

Bandy, Thomas. *Coaching Change.* Nashville: Abingdon, 2000.

Banks, Robert, and Bernice Ledbetter. *Receiving Leadership.* Grand Rapids: Baker, 2004.

Barna, George. *The Second Coming of the Church.* Nashville: Word, 1998.

*Highly recommended

————. *The Power of Team Leadership*. Colorado Springs: WaterBrook, 2005.

Bennis, Warren, Gretchen M. Spreitzer and Thomas G. Cummings, eds. *The Future of Leadership*. San Francisco: Jossey-Bass, 2001.

Berquist, William. *The Postmodern Organization*. San Francisco: Jossey-Bass, 1993.

Blanchard, Ken. *Leading at a Higher Level*. Upper Saddle River, N.J.: Prentice-Hall, 2006.

Blanchard, Ken, and Phil Hodges. *Lead Like Jesus*. Nashville: W Publishing, 2006.

Bradford, David, and Allan Cohen. *Power Up: Transforming Organizations Through Shared Leadership*. New York: Wiley & Sons, 1998.

Brafman, Ori, and Rod Beckstrom. *The Starfish and the Spider: The Unstoppable Power of Leaderless Organizations*. New York: Penguin, 2006.

Brewin, Kester. *Signs of Emergence*. Grand Rapids: Baker, 2007.

Bridges, William, and Mitchell Bridges. "Leading Transition: A New Model for Change." *Leader to Leader* (spring 2000): 1-8.

Bultman, Bud. *Revolution by Candlelight*. Sisters, Ore.: Multnomah, 1991.

Bunker, Kerry. "Leading in Times of Transition." *Leading Effectively,* October 2005.

Burke, H. Dale. "Even Healthy Churches Need to Change." *Leadership* (fall 2005): 43-46.

*Burke, John. *No Perfect People Allowed*. Grand Rapids: Zondervan, 2005.

Burke, Spencer. *Making Sense of Church*. Grand Rapids: Zondervan, 2003.

Bush, George. "Our Society Rests on a Foundation of Responsibility." *USA Today,* September 3, 2004, p. 7A.

Callahan, Kennon. "The New Reality in Motivation." *Leadership* (fall 1999): 31-32.

Cartmill, Carol. "Don't Call Me a Leader." *Leadership* (summer 2003): 8.

*Carucci, Ron. *Leadership Divided: What Emerging Leaders Need and What You Might Be Missing*. San Francisco: Jossey-Bass, 2006.

Childress, Carol. "Roadshow 2000." *Explorer,* March 13, 2000, pp. 1-5.

Cleveland, Harlan. *Nobody in Charge*. San Francisco: Jossey-Bass, 2002.

Clinton, Robert. "Robert Clinton on Leadership." *Explorer,* January 3, 2000, pp. 1-3.

Collins, Gary. "An Integration View." In *Psychology and Christianity.* Edited by Eric Johnson and Stanton Jones. Downers Grove, Ill.: InterVarsity Press, 2000.

*Collins, Jim. *Good to Great*. New York: HarperCollins, 2001.

————. *Good to Great and the Social Sectors*. Boulder, Colo.: Jim Collins, 2005.

————. "Level 5 Leadership: The Triumph of Humility and Fierce Resolve." In
    Harvard Business Review (January 2001): 67-76.

————. "What Comes Next?" *Inc.,* October 1997, pp. 41-49.

Conder, Tim. *The Church in Transition.* Grand Rapids: Zondervan, 2006.

Conlin, Michelle. "Cheating or Postmodern Learning." *Business Week,* May 14,
    2007, p. 42.

Conner, Daryl. *Leading at the Edge of Chaos.* New York: Wiley & Sons, 1998.

Dale, Robert. *Leadership for a Changing Church.* Nashville: Abingdon, 1998.

De Pree, Max. *Leadership Is an Art.* East Lansing: Michigan State University Press,
    1987.

*————. *Leading Without Power.* San Francisco: Jossey-Bass, 1997.

Dickens, Charles. *A Tale of Two Cities.* 1859. Reprint, New York: Modern Library,
    1950.

Dickens, Peter. "Incarnational Leadership in a Postmodern Culture" (unpublished
    paper).

Earls, Alan. "Clash of Generations in Workplace." *Boston Globe,* August 10, 2003,
    pp. 1G, 7G.

Easum, Bill. *Sacred Cows Make Great Gourmet Burgers.* Nashville: Abingdon, 1995.

————. *Leadership on the Other Side.* Nashville: Abingdon, 2000.

Easum, Bill, and Dave Travis. *Beyond the Box.* Loveland, Colo.: Group, 2003.

"Effective Churches and Team Leadership." *Next* 5, no. 3 (1999): 1.

Essentials of Management: Participant Workbook. New York: American Management
    Association, 1977.

Fletcher, Joyce. "The Greatly Exaggerated Demise of Heroic Leadership." *Center for
    Gender in Organizations Insights,* August 2002, pp. 1-4.

*Ford, Kevin. *Transforming Church.* Carol Stream Ill.: Tyndale, 2007.

————. *Transforming Leadership.* Downers Grove, Ill.: InterVarsity Press, 1991.

Ford, Kevin, and James Osterhaus. *The Thing in the Bushes.* Colorado Springs:
    Piñon, 2001.

Ford, Leighton. "Challenges in Nurturing and Forming Leaders for 2010," Evan-
    gelical Foreign Missions Association conference address, September 21, 1999.

Ford, Paul. "From My Vision to Our Vision." *Leadership* (summer 2000): 34-38.

Forman, Rowland, Jeff Jones and Bruce Miller. *The Leadership Baton.* Grand Rapids:
    Zondervan, 2004.

Foss, Mike. "Authentic Leadership and the Call of God." *Next* 5, no. 4 (1999): 1-2.

Frost, Michael, and Alan Hirsch. *The Shape of Things to Come*. Peabody, Mass.: Hendrickson, 2003.

Fryling, Robert. "When Leaders Fear Risk," pp. 1-3. In *Student Leadership*. Madison, Wis.: IVCF, 1988.

*George, Bill. *True North: Discover Your Authentic Leadership*. San Francisco: Wiley & Sons, 2007.

George, Rusty, and Jeff Krajewski. *Herding Cats*. Joplin, Mo.: College Press, 2001.

*Gibbs, Eddie. *LeadershipNext*. Downers Grove, Ill.: InterVarsity Press, 2005.

Gibbs, Eddie, and Ryan Bolger. *Emerging Churches*. Grand Rapids: Baker Academic, 2005.

Gill, Robin. *Moral Leadership in a Postmodern Age*. Edinburgh: T & T Clark, 1997.

Goethals, George, Georgia J. Sorenson and James MacGregor Burns, eds. *Encyclopedia of Leadership*. Thousand Oaks, Calif.: Sage, 2004.

Goffee, Rob, and Gareth Jones. "Managing Authenticity: The Paradox of Great Leadership." *Harvard Business Review* (December 2005): 87-94.

―――. "The Price and Prize of Leadership," *Leader to Leader* (fall 2006): 41-46.

―――. "What Holds the Modern Company Together." *Harvard Business Review* (November–December 1996): 133-48.

―――. *Why Should Anyone Be Led by You?* Boston: Harvard Business School Press, 2003.

Goldsmith, Marshall. "Leading New Age Professionals." In *The Leader of the Future 2*. Edited by Frances Hesselbein and Marshall Goldsmith. San Francisco: Jossey-Bass, 2006.

Greenleaf, Robert. *Servant Leadership*. New York: Paulist, 1977.

―――. *The Servant As Leader*. Peterborough, N.H.: Windy Row, 1970.

Gunderson, Denny. "Leadership in a Postmodern World." *Mars Hill Review* 12 (fall 1998): 51-54.

Hall, Chad. "Leader's Insight: NASCAR and the Emerging Culture." Leadership Journal.net <http://www.christianitytoday.com/leaders/newsletter/2005/cln51017.html>, October 17, 2005.

Handy, Charles. *The Age of Paradox*. Boston: Harvard Business School Press, 1994.

————. *The Age of Unreason*. Boston: Harvard Business School Press, 1989.

*Heifetz, Ronald, and Marty Linsky. *Leadership on the Line*. Boston: Harvard Business School Press, 2005.

Helgesen, Sally. "Challenge for Leaders in the Years Ahead." In *The Leader of the Future 2*. Edited by Frances Hesselbein and Marshall Goldsmith. San Francisco: Jossey-Bass, 2006.

Hesselbein, Frances, "Know Thy Times." *Leader to Leader* (fall 2006): 4-6.

————. "The Leaders We Need." *Leader to Leader* (winter 2005): 1-5.

Hesselbein, Frances, and Marshall Goldsmith, ed. *The Leader of the Future 2*. San Francisco: Jossey-Bass, 2006.

Hesselbein, Frances, and Rob Johnston. *On Leading Change*. San Francisco: Jossey-Bass, 2002.

————. *On Mission and Leadership*. San Francisco: Jossey-Bass, 2002.

*Hesselbein, Frances, ed. *The Leader of the Future*. San Francisco: Jossey-Bass, 1996.

————. *Leading Beyond the Walls*. San Francisco: Jossey-Bass, 1999.

Hesselbein, Frances, et al. *The Community of the Future*. San Francisco: Jossey-Bass, 1998.

————. *The Organization of the Future*. San Francisco: Jossey-Bass, 1997.

Hickman, Gill Robinson, ed. *Leading Organizations: Perspectives for a New Era*. Thousand Oaks, Calif.: Sage, 1998.

Hilland, Roger. "Nothing Leadership." Allelon Institute Article, January 2006 newsletter.

Hira, Nadira. "Attracting the Twentysomething Worker." *Fortune,* May 15, 2008.

Hirschhorn, Larry. *Reworking Authority: Leading and Following in the Post-Modern Organization*. Cambridge, Mass.: MIT Press, 1997.

*Hjalmarson, Len. "Kingdom Leadership in the Postmodern World." Next Reformation <http://nextreformation.com/wp-admin/resources/Leadership.pdf>.

Hock, Dee. "The Art of Chaotic Leadership." *Leader to Leader* (winter 2000): 20-26.

Huey, John. "The New Post-Heroic Leaderhip." *Fortune,* February 21, 1994, pp. 42-50.

Hughes, Donald. "The Leadership Model of Jesus." JesusJournal.com <http://www.jesusjournal.com/content/view/90/85/>.

Hunsberger, George. "Leaders in the Missional Church." *The Gospel and Our Culture* 10, no. 2 (1998): 6-7.

Hunter, James. *The World's Most Powerful Leadership Principle.* Colorado Springs: WaterBrook, 2004.

Ireland, Duane, and Michael Hilt. "Achieving and Maintaining Strategic Competitiveness in the 21st Century: The Role of Strategic Leadership." *Academy of Management Executive* 13, no. 1 (1999): 43-57.

Jethani, Skye. "Next and Level: A Leadership Interview." *Leadership* (spring 2008): 25-29.

*Keel, Timothy. *Intuitive Leadership: Embracing a Paradigm of Narrative Metaphor and Chaos.* Grand Rapids: Baker, 2007.

———. "Leading from the Margins." In *An Emergent Manifesto of Hope.* Edited by Doug Pagitt and Tony Jones. Grand Rapids: Baker, 2007.

Kelly, Gerard. *Get a Grip on the Future Without Losing Your Hold on the Past.* London: Monarch, 1999.

———. *RetroFuture: Rediscovering Our Roots, Recharting Our Routes.* Downers Grove, Ill.: InterVarsity Press, 1999.

Kennedy, Marilyn Moats. "Managing the Deliberately Mute." *Physician Executive* (January-February 2000): 68-70.

Kimball, Dan. *The Emerging Church.* Grand Rapids: Zondervan, 2002.

Kohut, Andrew. "How Young People View Their Lives, Futures and Politics: A Portrait of Generation Next." Pew Research Center, 2006.

Kotter, John. *Leading Change.* Boston: Harvard Business School Press, 1996.

———. "What Leaders Really Do." *Harvard Business Review on Leadership.* Cambridge, Mass.: Harvard Business School Press, 1998.

Kouzes, James, and Barry Posner. *Christian Reflections on Leadership Challenge.* San Francisco: Jossey-Bass, 2004.

———. "It's Not Just the Leader's Vision." In *The Leader of the Future 2.* Edited by Frances Hesselbein and Marshall Goldsmith. San Francisco: Jossey-Bass, 2006.

Lencioni, Patrick. "The Trouble with Teamwork." *Leader to Leader* (summer 2003): 35-40.

Lewis, Robert, and Wayne Cordeiro. *Culture Shift.* San Francisco: Jossey-Bass, 2005.

Licitra, Annette. "Linux's Quiet Leader Courts Success." *Executive Leadership*, (2008): 4.

Long, Jimmy. *Emerging Culture Curriculum Kit*. Downers Grove, Ill.: InterVarsity Press, 2004.

————. *Emerging Hope: A Strategy for Reaching Postmodern Generations*. Downers Grove, Ill.: InterVarsity Press, 2004.

MacDonald, Gordon. *Who Stole My Church?* Nashville: Thomas Nelson, 2007.

Martoia, Ron. *Morph: The Texture of Leadership for Tomorrow's Church*. Loveland, Colo.: Group, 2003.

Maske, Mark. "Toned Down Coughlin Helped Giants Turn It Up." *Washington Post*, January 20, 2008, p. D1.

Mayo, Anthony, and Nitin Nohria. "Zeitgeist Leadership." *Harvard Business Review* (October 2005): 45-60.

McCorty, Leroy. "The Humble Leader." Emergingleader.com <http://www.emergingleader.com/article20.shtml>.

McLaren, Brian. *The Church on the Other Side*. Grand Rapids: Zondervan, 2000.

————. "Dorothy on Leadership." *Rev!* November-December 2000.

McManus, Alex. "New Leaders, Unmarked Paths." *Leadership* (summer 2003): 40-41.

McManus, Erwin. *An Unstoppable Force*. Loveland, Colo.: Group, 2001.

McNeal, Reggie. "Getting Real." *Next* 5 no. 4 (1999): 3-4.

————. *The Present Future*. San Francisco: Jossey-Bass, 2003.

Miller, Rex. *The Millennium Matrix*. San Francisco: Jossey-Bass, 2004.

Minatree, Milfred. *Shaped by God's Heart*. San Francisco: Jossey-Bass, 2004.

Monroe, Theresa. "Boundaries and Authenticity." In *Encyclopedia of Leadership*. Edited by George R. Goethals, Georgia J. Sorenson and James MacGregor Burns. Thousand Oaks, Calif.: Sage, 2004.

Morgenthaler, Sally. "Leadership in a Flattened World." In *An Emergent Manifesto of Hope*. Edited by Doug Pagitt and Tony Jones. Grand Rapids: Baker, 2007.

Myers, Joseph. *Organic Community*. Grand Rapids: Baker, 2007.

Netfax. Interview with George Cladis, "Leading the Team-Based Church." Leadership Network <https://www.leadnet.org/archives/netfax/120.pdf>, March 29, 1999.

Netfax. "The Three L's . . . Leadership, Learning and Listening." Leadership Network <https://www.leadnet.org/archives/netfax/122.pdf>, April 23, 1999.

Nouwen, Henri. *In the Name of Jesus.* New York: Crossroad, 1989.

―――. *The Wounded Healer.* New York: Doubleday, 1979.

Offerman, Lynn. "Empowerment." In *Encyclopedia of Leadership.* Edited by George R. Goethals, Georgia J. Sorenson and James MacGregor Burns. Thousand Oaks, Calif.: Sage, 2004.

O'Keefe, John. "A Postmodern Narrator." The OOZE <http://www.theooze.com/articles/article.cfm?id=366&page=1>, November 8, 2008.

Ortberg, Nancy. "Ministry Team Diagnostics." *Leadership* (spring 2008): 41-44.

―――. "Reflections on Enabling Others to Act." In *Christian Reflections on Leadership Challenge.* Edited by James Kouzes and Barry Posner. San Francisco: Jossey-Bass, 2004.

Osterhaus, Jim. "The New Bottom Line: Building a Relationally Healthy Organization." *Tagline* 1, no. 1 (2002): 1-2.

Osterhaus, James, et al. *Thriving Through Ministry Conflict.* Grand Rapids: Zondervan, 2005.

Pantoja, Dann. "Teaching Gen-Why?" *Leadership* (summer 2003): 48-51.

Pearce, Craig. "Share Leadership." In *Encyclopedia of Leadership.* Edited by George R. Goethals, Georgia J. Sorenson and James MacGregor Burns. Thousand Oaks, Calif.: Sage, 2004.

Raschke, Carl. *The Next Reformation.* Grand Rapids: Baker, 2004.

Roberts, Randall. *Lessons in Leadership.* Grand Rapids: Kregel, 1999.

Rodin, Scott. "Becoming a Leader of No Reputation" (unpublished paper).

Roxburgh, Alan. *The Missionary Congregation, Leadership and Luminality.* Harrisonburg, Penn.: Trinity Press International, 1997.

―――. *The Sky Is Falling.* Eagle, Idaho: ACI Publishing, 2006.

*Roxburgh, Alan, and Fred Romanuk. *The Missional Leader.* San Francisco: Jossey-Bass, 2006.

Sanders, Irene. *Strategic Thinking and the New Science.* New York: Free Press, 1998.

Sandmann, Lorilee R., and Lela Vandenberg. "A Framework for 21st Century Leadership." *Journal of Extension* 33, no. 6 (1995): 1-9

Schein, Edgar. *Organizational Culture and Leadership.* San Francisco: Jossey-Bass, 1992.

Schmidt, Henry. "Leadership in a Postmodern World." *Touch* (summer 2004): 1-3.

Schmotzer, Jim. "Leader's Insight: Bringing Milli's into Leadership." Christianity Today.com <http://www.christianitytoday.com/leaders/newsletter/2006/cln60227.html>, February 27, 2006.

Schoenberg, Nana. "Teens Embracing Hugging Trend." *Raleigh News and Observer,* October 10, 2007, p. E14.

Senge, Peter. *The Fifth Discipline: The Art and Practice of the Learning Organization.* New York: Doubleday, 1990.

———. "Leading, Learning and Organizing." *Explorer,* June 19, 2000, pp. 1-4.

*———. *Presence.* New York: Doubleday, 2004.

Shelley, Marshall. "State of the Art: An Interview with Andy Stanley." *Leadership* (spring 2006): 26-32.

Spears, Larry. "Practicing Servant Leadership." *Leader to Leader* (fall 2004): 1-6.

Springle, Pat. "Communications with the Postmodern Culture," A Leadership Network Paper, 2007 <www.leadnet.org/downloads/Communicating%20With%20the%20Postmodern%20Culture.pdf>.

———. "Creating a Culture of Balance," A Leadership Network Paper, 2007 <www.leadnet.org/downloads/file_400.pdf>.

Stanley, Andy. *The Next Generation Leader.* Sisters, Ore.: Multnomah, 2003.

Stott, John. *Basic Christian Leadership.* Downers Grove, Ill.: InterVarsity Press, 2002.

Sweet, Leonard. *Aqua Church.* Loveland, Colo.: Group, 1999.

———. "New Maps for an Ancient Future." *Explorer,* June 10, 2000, pp. 5-11.

———. *Soul Tsunami.* Grand Rapids: Zondervan, 1999.

———. *Summoned to Lead.* Grand Rapids: Zondervan, 2004.

Tiplady, Richard. *Postmission: World Mission by a Postmodern Generation.* London: Paternoster, 2002.

Tokunaga, Paul. *Invitation to Lead.* Downers Grove, Ill.: InterVarsity Press, 2003.

Wallace, William. *Postmodern Management.* London: Quorum, 1998.

Ward, Angie. "Better Starts for Emerging Leaders." Christianity Today.com <http://www.christianitytoday.com/leaders/newsletter/2004/cln40720.html>, July 20, 2004.

———. "Looking for Leaders." *Leadership* (spring 2006): 19-22.

Waterman, Robert. *The Renewal Factor.* New York: Bantam, 1987.

Webber, Robert. *The Younger Evangelicals.* Grand Rapids: Baker, 2002.

Wetlaufer, Suzy. "Organizing for Empowerment: An Interview with AES's Roger Sant and Dennis Bakke." *Harvard Business Review* (January–February 1999): 111-23.

*Wheatley, Margaret. *Finding Our Way: Leadership for an Uncertain Time.* San Francisco: Berrett-Koehler, 2005.

———. "Goodbye, Command and Control." *Leader to Leader* (summer 1997): 21-28.

———. "The Real Work of Leadership." *Explorer,* May 8, 2000, pp. 1-3.

White, Randall. *The Future of Leadership.* Lanham, Md.: Pittman, 1996.

*Wright, Walter. *Don't Step on the Rope.* Bletchley, U.K.: Paternoster, 2005.

Zolar, Danah. "Spiritually Intelligent Leadership." *Leader to Leader* (fall 2005): 1-8.

Zust, Christine. "The Compassionate Leader." Emergingleader.com <http://www.emergingleader.com/article19.shtml>.

———. "How Leaders Can Command, Not Demand, Respect." Emergingleader .com <http://www.emergingleader.com/article24.shtml>.